ULTIMATE BOAT MAINTENANCE PROJECTS

12/06

ULTIMATE *BOAT* MAINTENANCE

PROJECTS

Scott "Sky" Smith

MOTORBOOKS
INTERNATIONAL

First published in 2004 by Motorbooks
International, an imprint of MBI Publishing
Company, Galtier Plaza, Suite 200, 380 Jackson
Street, St. Paul, MN 55101-3885 USA.

Motorbooks International titles are also available at
discounts in bulk quantity for industrial or sales-
promotional use. For details write to the Special
Sales Manager at Motorbooks International
Wholesalers & Distributors, Galtier Plaza, Suite 200,
380 Jackson Street, St. Paul, MN 55101-3885 USA.

ISBN 0-7603-1696-1

Aquisition Editor: Dennis Pernu
Editor: Chad Caruthers
Layout: Chris Fayers

Printed in China

Contents

Acknowledgments

No matter what anyone says, it takes more than one person to write a book, any book. Now is the time for thanks. I thank my wife, my business and life partner, Jeanne for helping me get the text and photographs organized, and for keeping me on task. An accomplished writer, business executive, and motivator, Jeanne was an invaluable asset. Thanks also needs to go to my kids Zach and Aerielle for their assistance in the photo shoots, and for helping at home and at the office so I had the free time needed for writing.

As an aviation and marine insurance agency owner, I have to acknowledge the assistance of my staff in helping me complete this book. Without them running the day-to-day operations of the business, I wouldn't have been able to spend the extra time necessary writing and gathering the information and photos.

Many thanks definitely go to Scott Hendricks and his family for their support, time, and the use of his boat when mine was not available. Good photography needs good preparation, and Scott was able to help get the projects in front of the camera.

Thanks to Steve Klein for the use of his shop and for additional photography when the weather got cold.

And I can't forget the local boat shops: The guys at Dave's Marine in Des Moines, Iowa, were always available when we needed advice or a few extra photos. Dave's only does maintenance, not fiberglass or paintwork, on boats.

Thanks also to the folks at Mau Marine, Inc., of Des Moines; they were a great help on additional maintenance items, including fiberglass and paintwork.

Even though this book is about owner maintenance (repairs that you don't have to take to the shop), the staff at Dave's Marine and Mau Marine was more than ready to help. Both shops have mechanics with years of experience. Their comments and workmanship are a great reminder of why some things are better left to the professionals.

Owner Bill Sprague does more maintenance than anyone else I know. He believes owner maintenance is one of the fun things about boat ownership. Thanks to Bill for sharing his experience.

Another thanks goes to the Martin Flory Group and, in particular, Amanda Bulgrin. The Martin Flory Group is a great public relations firm that provided me with a number of helpful contacts in the marine industry.

Numerous other manufacturers and dealers have provided information and products for use in the book. A thanks goes out to all of them for their enthusiasm and assistance to help owners learn a little more about their boats and make the projects go a little easier. I hope I didn't forget any of you!

Introduction

Speed, fishing, or just floating in the sun—boating is a sport for the whole family. *Bill Fedorko*

Why do your own maintenance? Let's talk about the boating world from its inception. When was the start? When was the first boat built? Was it a canoe, a raft, or a first-edition V-bottom vessel? We might not ever know what was the first actual boat design. For as long as people can remember, boats have been a mode of transportation anywhere on the earth. It appears that the boat can be traced back to almost the "recorded" beginning of time. Ancient scrolls and biblical references were made to boats. Noah was reported to have rescued mankind in an ark (was this the first cargo ship?) that floated across the water and ran aground in a land yet undiscovered. Travelers in ships discovered many of the continents. From the Norse Vikings to the Spanish explorers, boats have been the transportation choice throughout history.

Mankind has used the waterways to travel countless miles. It has used vessels of all shapes, sizes, and types of power. Oceans cover over three-fourths of our planet's surface. The human body is made up of over 70 percent water. That makes water one of the most, if not *the* most, valuable resources for living, working, and playing. Maybe man was the first water vessel—when he swam the first river. Regardless, water travel has been around for a long, long time.

Looking at the evolution of travel, water appears to lead the transportation revolution, except for man's own two feet. Travel today is by land, sea, or air. Man didn't travel by the horseless carriage until the late

1800s. Powered flight didn't occur until 1903. Sure, the wheel was invented before the powered automobile, but what came before the wheel? The boat. Thus, boats may be the oldest man-made mode of travel.

If it is such a prominent means of transportation, why doesn't everyone own a boat? There are, in fact, more than 71 million pleasure boaters, the people who participate in recreational boating activities, and this book is designed for them. According to the National Marine Manufacturers Association (NMMA), there were over 17.3 million pleasure boats on the registries in the year 2002. The NMMA also estimates that there are over 94,000 watercraft listed for sale at any given time.

How do these numbers compare historically? The NMMA estimates that in 1913 there were approximately 400,000 recreational boats. The industry took a big jump in the 1930s, with about 1.5 million boats, and another major jump in the 1980s to about 11 million recreational boats. While the subsequent years saw significantly smaller increases, the fact that there are more than 17 million boats today indicates that pleasure boating is a huge market.

So, there are a lot of boats. What does that have to do with boat-owner maintenance and service? With that many boats on the water, you'd think that getting your boat serviced would be a cinch. However, it is estimated that there are only about 4,500 official marine dealers in the United States. That's only one dealer for every 3,800 boats. While there are numerous marine service and repair shops around the country that are not marine dealers, there is still more demand for these services than the supply of shops can accommodate. In addition, not all boats are within close proximity to one of these shops. After talking with a few repair shops, the consensus is that there is no way they can maintain all the boats that are being used in their area. With far more boats than service or repair centers, repairs can take longer than expected or parts might be difficult to get.

The cost of purchasing and servicing a boat is another aspect that underlines the need for boat-owner maintenance. A boat needs to be thought of as an investment, and a boat owner should ultimately expect some form of return on this investment. With over 17 million boats, the market resale value for a boat can be tough to maintain. If you want your boat to maintain its value, proper maintenance is essential. To own is to maintain. Maintenance doesn't necessarily mean the owner needs to do *everything* for the boat. In fact, a good boat-maintenance facility is still the best choice for most boat-owner maintenance.

However, in many cases owners prefer to perform their own maintenance. It is their boat, it's their time, and they like to do their own work on their boat. It's a part of ownership that can actually be *fun*. It is part of the experience and pride of ownership, like owning a collectible car, motorcycle, or even an aircraft. While we can't all be mechanics, we can all do a few things to keep our boat in the best shape possible and give us, the owners, a feeling of accomplishment.

Even with my background—growing up in a marina, teaching auto mechanics, working in a fiberglass-boat manufacturing plant—there are things I do not like to do. I enjoy refinishing fiberglass, paintwork, and basic engine maintenance, but I do not like detailing the boat, cleaning the small crevices with a toothbrush, and the like. So I have gotten in the habit of doing the things I like and hiring someone to do the things that I don't enjoy.

Regardless of the maintenance you enjoy or dislike performing, there are certain things that an owner needs to know how to do. Doing your own maintenance can increase your knowledge of the basic systems in the boat, and by developing a better understanding of the systems, you can help give a better explanation of the problem so a mechanic can diagnose the problem when something does go wrong. Also consider that if you're ever stranded, waiting hours for a tow and service, only to discover that the problem was something very basic, you will realize the importance of knowing your boat. A minor repair that can help you limp back to the dock can save you hours of time, a lot of money, and it may even be safer than waiting in the water for assistance.

A recent study indicates that the U.S. boating market is going through a change. Boat owners are starting to expect the same treatment that they receive from their automobile dealer. They expect to take their vehicle into the shop and have it repaired quickly and economically. However, the reality is that the average service takes an estimated two days, which quickly turns into four days . . .

Part of the problem is that the smaller shops are unable to keep an inventory of parts for the ever-changing boat and engine models. That means the order time of parts and supplies at the smaller shops slows down the service turnaround time. To accommodate boat owners' demand for the automotive-service experience, the marine industry needs to improve its service experience dramatically to maintain customers. There are always going to be new boaters, but how long they stay in the market will be based on how satisfied they are with the overall experience, and that includes the products and the service.

While these examples alone make a strong case for owner maintenance, add in that it can actually reduce the stress of ownership as well as maintain the market value and usability of the boat. Well-maintained boats usually bring more money on the used market. Well-maintained boats break down less on the water. Well-maintained boats cost less in the long run because they are operating at a higher efficiency. And when an owner sells the boat, it will have maintained its used market value better than a decrepit, neglected pile of fiberglass and dust.

If, however, your boat is over 20 years old, it can be hard to find parts or, in some cases, impossible. Even if it is well maintained and a good runner, if the manufacturer is out of business, service and parts can be difficult to acquire. Dealer support on old equipment is almost nonexistent. Therefore, owner maintenance is the only way to keep it running. When it comes to irreplaceable parts, a boat owner must find serviceable used parts or, in some cases, may simply need to upgrade to a newer model.

For certain, there are a lot of boats on the water and not enough professionals to service them all. Now is the perfect time to learn about and perform proper boat maintenance. That's what this book is all about. This is not a detailed service manual for any particular boat or engine; it is a generic guide for the owner to maintain his or her boat as a dealer or service person would. It's broken down into a few basic areas, bow to stern.

You'll learn how to perform the preventive maintenance needed to keep your boat in top-notch condition, with results including improved performance, lower operating costs, and a better resale value. Most of the projects in this book can be done with regular tools and without any special skills. Again, this is not meant as a replacement for your local mechanic. It is also not going to be the only way to do any of these service items. Many mechanics and owners have developed their own techniques. These are just a few things that can help you get the process started.

Not all of the photos in this book go in a direct sequence or are even from the same project boat, while some of the work shown was started on a red boat and the finished views are of a green boat. This setup was intentional. The idea is to show you what the project might look like on another type of boat or engine.

Finally, remember that this book is not designed to replace your dealership or favorite mechanic. It is intended to be an enhancement to your boat maintenance and ownership. In certain situations, your mechanic can save you time and money on maintenance items and projects. A smart owner knows what he or she can do, and what else needs to be left to the professional.

It doesn't matter if you have an inboard, outboard, or an inboard/outboard boat. This book offers the basic techniques needed to do preventive maintenance for your boat.

Tool and Safety Tips

I like a well-equipped shop, whether I use all the tools regularly or not. I've never been one to borrow or rent tools. I like to own. If possible, instead of investing in new tools right away, take a look at the cost and the frequency you think you will use a tool compared to the cost of having a mechanic do the service.

For example, the average boat will probably have one oil change per season. It's a pretty basic maintenance project for the owner to undertake, but it is a good idea to purchase Tempo's Oil Boy Fluid Extractor Kit, which is $60. Add to that the cost of the oil and filters, $22. Finally, budget $20 for driving around, finding a recycling center, and paying to dispose of the used oil. The total: $102. The pump is reusable, so subsequent self-performed oil changes should cost around $42. Shops charge between $40 and $75, plus oil and filter. That means you could pay a shop $62 to $97 per oil change. The wild card is the amount of time you have available to perform such projects. Depending on how much your time is worth, it might be "cheaper" to let the shop do the oil change. That's for you to decide. Regardless, a cost

Klein Tools offers a Tool Tote that will hold most of the necessary hand tools for your marine projects. In addition to the handy tool pockets on the outside, I put my assorted sockets, ratchets, wrenches, and cordless tools in the open center of the Tool Tote.

analysis should be undertaken for each project you are considering.

Make sure you have a copy of the boat's owner's manual, and a service and parts manual. You should also have a copy of the service and parts manual for the engine and stern drive or the outboard motor. These items are going to be vital resources regarding your particular boat and engine. The manufacturers recommend certain times for individual services and specific products for your boat and engine. For the best life and continued warranty service, it's always best to follow the manufacturer's guidelines.

Any basic toolbox should be equipped with enough tools to complete most of the projects in this book. There are a couple of specialized tools, like an oil-change pump, that make the chore easier and cleaner, but they are not a necessity. The average boat owner doesn't need the top-of-the-line tool or every imaginable tool designed. What an owner needs is a few quality, basic tools. A prepackaged set is a pretty good way to buy your tools. Although different boats and engines require different tools, you can't go

Electricity and water don't mix. Cordless tools provide an added level of safety by eliminating the need for extension cords, and reducing the risk of electrocution.

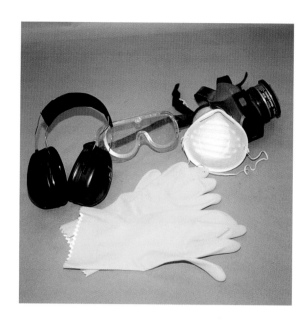

Boat maintenance can create safety issues that can be alleviated with common household safety equipment to protect your hearing, eyesight, respiratory system, and skin.

wrong if you have an assorted set of screwdrivers, nut drivers (or a nut-driver handle and assorted small sockets), pliers, long-nose pliers, diagonal cutters, sharp knife, wire strippers, adjustable wrench, small set of sockets, extension and ratchet with a spark plug socket for your engine, a set of combination wrenches (the ratcheting kind are nice but not necessary), and a small hammer. Kits with these types of tools can be purchased for less than $30. Other gadgets are helpful and fun to use, but not necessary. Always be certain to buy quality tools, keep them clean, and ensure they are in good condition.

Part of basic maintenance is cleaning, so if you don't have a gallon bucket, buy one, as well as a quality garden hose and a spray nozzle. A power washer can be of value if you have one, but it isn't necessary. In addition, include cleaning and finishing products—such as carpet and fabric cleaner, carnauba-based marine paste wax—as part of your maintenance supplies.

Buy a high-quality and easy-to-carry wet/dry vacuum. This is one area where a corded version is probably the best. The power of a small rechargeable unit just doesn't seem to do the trick.

Sound can be harmful to your ears, whether it be from a vacuum, your boat's engine, or the wind whistling in your ears. Purchase some quality earplugs to protect your hearing. Make sure you get a brand and decibel-reduction rating that is going to work for you.

Some of the items used to clean the boat are hazardous. Wear eye protection whenever possible. Power buffers, sanders, and sprayers can throw debris and chemicals back into your eyes. Lightweight rubber gloves can protect your skin when applying chemicals to clean the hull or fabric in the cabin.

You will also need a quality indoor-outdoor extension cord. The length will be up to you and your situation. Make sure the cord and the outlet are both grounded for protection. Do not use a cord that has the third grounding plug removed. Use indoor cords indoors only. Keep all cords away from and out of the water. In addition, a few-hundred-watt portable generator, if you need one, will suffice for most of the work on your boat.

For this reason, and for other matters of convenience, consider purchasing cordless tools. A good cordless tool kit should include some sort of cordless drill/screwdriver that can be used as a buffer and sander. Bosch Tools makes a very good, compact 3/8-inch, 14.4-volt cordless drill/driver, the Compact Tough. One big advantage of the Bosch is its small size. The 14.4-volt rechargeable battery lasts quite a while, and if you need to charge it, you can connect it to a power converter in your vehicle. Purchase a 5-inch hook and loop pad (with the buffing pad and sanding disks) at a hardware store, and you can go from a soft buffing pad to a sanding disk in seconds.

Blocking the tires on the trailer will prevent the trailer from inadvertently moving while you are working on your boat or trailer.

Dirt and moisture damage boats. A quality wet/dry vacuum is a necessity. A few cordless models are available, but they do not offer the suction needed like that from the Shop Vac.

To prevent the boat/trailer from tipping on its lower unit, place a jack (or safety) stand under the rear of the trailer, against the trailer frame.

I also like the small, cordless 10.8-volt model Dremel tool that can be used to wire-brush small areas on cleats and fittings, or grind small chips and cracks to prepare them for filling. You can use a Dremel for cleaning spark plugs, threads on bolts, and bolt holes as well. Since it is cordless and small, it can be used in a lot of areas that the larger tools cannot. The Dremel can even be fitted with additional attachments and used for other jobs that you would normally need a shop full of tools to complete. The right-angle attachment will allow you to sand or grind an area that won't allow direct, straight-in access for the Dremel. A flex-shaft attachment will allow the bit to be maneuvered into hard-to-reach areas. The multipurpose cutting kit turns the Dremel into a rotary saw, using a straight bit that allows holes to be made when a circular saw or jigsaw is too big. Dremel even makes a Mini Saw, which has a small saw blade that can be used to cut wood and fiberglass. Rarely have I needed more power than what the 10.8-volt Dremel provides, and I like its simplicity.

Any painting or cleaning can cause fumes that can be hazardous. An appropriate air-filter mask should be worn at all times. Painting and polishing should always be done in a well-ventilated area. Make sure there are no open flames, such as pilot lights and furnaces, in the area you are painting or when you are working with the fuel system. Disconnect the battery at the battery to eliminate the risk of fire or explosion. Always store fuel in approved and appropriately marked containers, away from an ignition source.

Boat trailers roll and move when you lean against or work on them, so it is important to secure the trailer. You can leave the trailer connected to your vehicle during the repairs. That keeps the trailer from tipping and stops the trailer from rolling. If you are working on the boat while the trailer is unhooked from the vehicle, block the front and back of the tire with a block of wood or premade wheel chocks. If you are climbing in and out of the boat, you should put blocks or a safety stand under the rear of the trailer to prevent it from tipping. Tipping not only damages the lower end, but it also damages your pride when all the other boaters start laughing.

So, it's time to roll up your sleeves, get out the toolbox, charge up your cordless tools, and get started.

SECTION 1

EXTERIOR
Projects 1 through 9

Not only will a clean and well-maintained exterior make you happy, but it is good for the boat. If you ever sell the boat, potential buyers will be impressed. While the interior, oil changes, or lower-end service may only be required once a year, the exterior is an area that should be cleaned and polished regularly. Since it is a regular project and actually one of the easiest for the owner, it's at the front of the list.

One of the best investments for a boat owner is a cordless drill/driver. The 14.4-volt Bosch Compact Tough that I use offers more than enough power for the owner maintenance items we cover in the book.

Any vehicle—whether it's a car, boat, or aircraft—can benefit from the cleaning of its exterior surfaces. The finish needs to be protected from the UV rays of the sunlight, harsh temperature changes, and the weather. Cleaning and waxing the exterior creates a smoother and better-looking finish. A smooth finish will make it harder for dirt and algae to bond to the surface and reduce the difficulty of cleaning the next time. The smoother, cleaner surface creates less drag in the water, which in turn should create a faster boat! Cleaning also gives you a chance to review the overall condition of the boat and look for spots that might need repair.

Like any other boat-service work, an owner can hire a professional service to clean and maintain the outside of the boat. Hiring a crew to lift the boat out of the water to clean and paint the bottom, while not a cheap task, is well worth the cost to me. On the larger vessels, hiring a crew that will clean the bottom while it is in the slip is a must.

Washing the exterior of a boat can cost anywhere from about $2 to about $5 per foot of length. The cost can go up if the hull is in need of a lot of cleaning (algae, barnacles, lots of scratches, etc.). Any kind of professional detailing service is going to charge you a lot more. Typically, the rates run from $15 to $20 a foot. A 30-foot hull length would be about $600. Yet, think about the associated costs. That's a pretty reasonable price considering the cost of the tools and the supplies needed to do a good cleaning.

Another very good purchase is a Dremel cordless tool kit. The cordless Dremel allows the owner to grind, sand, polish and more . . . it's cordless and works in small confined spaces. The Dremel will work on almost every part of the boat, as long as the area is not very big. This is a tool for small operations.

There are more items on the exterior than just the cleaning of the finish and a coat of wax. A boat that is used will get chips, cracks, scratches, and other finish problems that need to be cleaned and repaired. An aluminum boat will get unsightly black streaks from metal pieces moving that could indicate loose rivets. The wood-trimmed ladders can become weak and fail from constant moisture. For safety, even the cleats, railings, and other fittings need some sort of care like cleaning and protecting the finish from corrosion. Holes, large cracks that have damaged the structure, or any other major repair should be done by a professional who has the equipment, knowledge, and materials.

Most boats, whether made of composite or wood, acquire nicks, scratches, and cracks. As an owner, it is important to make sure you inspect the boat and look for as many of the imperfections as you can find and try to correct them.

Some scratches are easy to remove. All you'll need is a little elbow grease, a soft cloth, and a polishing compound. A power buffer can save you hours of hand-polishing, but it also requires access to electricity.

A cordless buffer offers portability, and free movement around the boat. The disadvantage comes in the lower RPMs for buffing. Cordless buffers, however, do provide satisfactory buffing ability.

By using cordless tools, waxing and polishing can be done right on the lift or trailer.

PROJECT 1 ★ *Minor Surface Scratches*

When: Beginning and end of season

Time: 2–4 hours (drying time, 24 hours)

Tools: Polish-applicator pad; clean, soft cloth; spreading paddle and small paintbrush; 600 (or higher) grit wet/dry sandpaper; sanding block

Supplies: Crest toothpaste; polishing compound; marine paste wax; factory-match touchup paint, model paint, or fingernail polish

Talent: ★★

Tab: Under $15–35

Tip: Do not sand a large area around the scratch; limit sanding to a small area. Non-gel toothpaste such as original Crest works the best on minor scratches

Gain: Improved look, better resale, longer life

It's recommended that any boat owner have a bottle of a very fine polishing compound (such as McGuire's) and a good paste wax on hand. Most of the discount stores (Wal-Mart, Kmart, etc.) or auto supply stores can provide you with a small container to be used for buffing out the tiny imperfections in the finish, and wax for putting that water-resistant shine back on the finish. Polishing and buffing compounds are a little different. Usually, buffing compounds are more abrasive and used to smooth a surface initially. Polishing is usually not abrasive and helps restore the oils and chemical in the paint or finish.

Our goal is to remove the scratches by buffing, sanding, or filling. Most minor surface scratches will need nothing more than a little polishing with a quality polish. Few will need a coarse buffing compound. If the scratches are quite pronounced, a very fine compound is the best for an owner to use. Anything

Sometimes it may be easier to grab a tube of toothpaste and rub out a small scratch using your finger or a soft cloth. Original Crest also removes light oxidation easily from the finish. It acts like a fine polish.

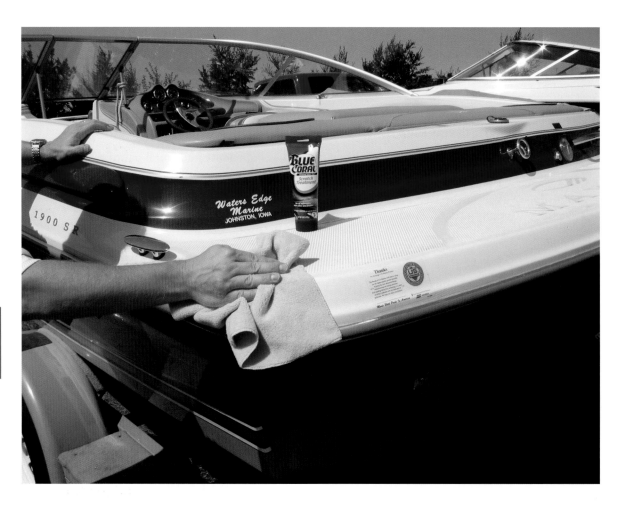

There are many commercial scratch removal treatments or pigmented polishes. Scratch removal products such as Blue Coral blend the surface colors to camouflage the scratch. Pigmented polishes fill the scratches with a blend of the paint surface and the polish. Always apply the products in small amounts and rub the scratch until it's not visible.

else can cause more damage than you started with. If you don't have access to a buffing compound, but still want to do a little scratch removal, try a tube of the original Crest toothpaste. Stay away from the gels and whitening toothpastes. What you are after is the fine, abrasive paste that will help remove the scratches.

Many small scratches in the finish can be removed by liberally applying the polishing compound (or Crest toothpaste) to the scratch and rubbing firmly with a soft cloth. If you are doing this by hand, do not rub too much of an area around the scratch. Crest toothpaste also will do a very good job removing oxidation from surfaces.

If the scratch has gone through the color (or the surface was painted), it's a different story. If the scratch is deep enough to show a different color, a fine buffing compound will not hide the scratch. It might smooth the finish, but the different color (usually a

lighter shade of the gel coat or white) will still be visible. Look for touchup paint, a pigmented polish, or a scratch treatment polish to hide the scratch. A pigmented waxing or polishing compound will help to blend the scratch to the current color. Quality scratch treatments like Blue Coral are not the cure-all for deep scratches, but for small past-the-color scratches, they do quite well. Beware if you are working with a clear coat; all it really does is blend the clear coat into the scratch. It actually might make it a different color than you want (more yellow than clear). Overall, I have had really good luck using Blue Coral and McGuire's scratch removal material.

Rub the pigmented polish into the scratch area with a soft cloth. The polish helps to blend the surface colors together and change the color of the scratched area to match the surface. Different manufacturers

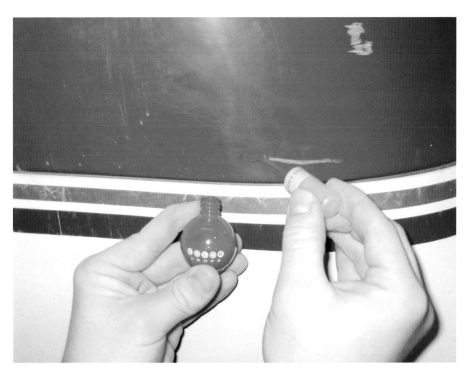

If the scratch is deep enough that a scratch treatment or pigmented polish won't remove it, then a good alternative is using touchup paint from the dealer, fingernail polish, or model paint to touch up a small scratch. With all the fingernail color options, it can be pretty easy to find a polish color that is close to the original color of the gel coat.

If the "small" scratch is deep enough to require filling, you can use a surface filler like glazing and spot putty or a gel-coat patch kit. Glazing putty is applied directly from the tube without additional additives. Painting will be required to hide the glazing putty.

talk about the way their polish adds oils and chemicals to rejuvenate the paint and bring life back into it. I think the thing to remember is that a good scratch treatment will hide the scratch; it might not ever remove it completely. Removal will need more than a surface treatment.

If the scratch is too deep to be camouflaged with the pigmented polish, you may need to apply a coat of paint. If you are painting the scratch with a color-matched paint, make sure you use a clean, small brush to apply the paint. Paint the scratch only, not the surrounding area. If you want to touch up the scratch, but do not have any of the touchup paint from the dealer or manufacturer, try using model paint (from a hobby store) or fingernail polish that is about the same color.

Sand the scratch with lots of clean water and very fine sandpaper. Using 600-grit on a sanding block will level the filled surface with the surrounding area. Any area you sand will need to be refinished, so keep the size of the sanded area as close to the scratch as possible. Use masking tape around any trim fittings or graphics to prevent unintentional damage.

If the scratch is in need of filling, a gel-coat repair kit can be used to add the colored gel coat directly to the scratch. Many small scratches can be filled using the Quick Fix Gel Coat Patch in a tube. There are other brands of filler available from marine supply stores. The advantage of this filler is that it doesn't need to be mixed, and it is applied directly from the tube to the scratch. Filler in a tube will not usually match the color of the gel coat. Most of the kits are white in color, and okay for hull repairs if the hull gel coat is white. You might have to buy the next step up, which is a gel-coat repair kit with a pigment to match the boat.

Spectrum Color provides a colored pigmented gel coat for almost every boat on the market. In our case, we needed a Four Winns red and white for a 1996 boat. Spectrum was able to provide a patch kit for the white (the patch kit is thicker and a smaller quantity) and a quart container of the red. The red needs to have filler added for large chips and cracks to thicken the material. Another advantage of the quart size is that it

allows us enough gel coat to spray colored gel coat over the repair. Spectrum also has a few great handbooks and "do-it-yourself" instructions available.

If you are planning on touching up the paint (and you have paint to match the boat finish), another easy-to-use filler is what's called "glazing putty," or surface scratch filler. This filler is from a tube that is spread over the scratch with a spreading paddle. This type of putty is made for very small scratches, pinholes, and grooves. *Do not* put on a thick coat. It needs to be used in very thin layers. After it's applied and allowed to dry, lightly sand the area with wet/dry sandpaper and a lot of freshwater. You will end up removing most of the filler, except what is in the scratch. Glazing putty will probably not match the color of the fiberglass or paint, so touchup painting is necessary.

If the hull color needs to be matched, make sure that you match the patch color to the original color of the finish, not the current faded color. After patching and sanding, the finish will fade and should look like the rest of the exterior in a number of months.

PROJECT 2 ★ *Filling Preparation*

When: Beginning and end of season

Time: 2–4 hours

Tools: Sandpaper (80-grit); masking or duct tape; razor knife; cordless Dremel tool and grinder bit

Supplies: Acetone

Talent: ★★★

Tab: $15–75

Tip: Make sure that the gel-coat filler is covered with plastic so it completely dries

Gain: Better adhesion of filler

If the area to be repaired is actually a big chipped area or a crack that needs to be filled, preparation will be the key to a good finish. It is very important to remove any wax or chemical buildup around the area. Do this by using a wax and grease remover, then rubbing with a clean cloth and acetone. Another alternative is lacquer thinner, both of which are available from most hardware or building supply stores. Of course, if the finish is painted, the acetone or thinner will remove the paint, so check to make sure you are cleaning the gel-coat finish, not a painted finish. After removing all the grease, wax, and grime from the scratch area, you will need to sand the area.

You should tape off the area so that the sanding of the surface is kept to a minimum. Most shops save the taping until they are ready to paint.

Remove any chips or pieces of gel coat that are loose. Sometimes it is necessary to chip or pry the surrounding area with a small pick or screwdriver. Loose edges need to be removed so the chipped area doesn't expand after you've done all the work. The crack can actually go under the surface of the gel coat, between the gel coat and fiberglass material. If you do not pick at it a little, the surrounding area of the patch may break loose and ruin the fresh patch.

Tape the areas that you don't want to get damaged. Most professionals use masking tape and masking paper. Owners can use masking tape or duct tape and a couple of sheets of newspaper. Duct tape protects the surface better, but often leaves a sticky residue. Newspaper needs to be doubled when painting because the sprayed material can bleed through the newsprint.

Larger scratches need to have any loose material removed (chips or flakes) and the area sanded into a bevel or "V" shape. It is very important to make the crack easy to fill. If you cannot get the filler into the bottom of the crack, there will always be an air pocket at the bottom and the filler will pop out sometime in the near future. I really like using my cordless Dremel with a small grinder bit to remove the loose pieces of gel coat and expand the area to get it ready for the filler. Remember to always wear eye protection when using the Dremel (or other power tools). This small Dremel tool can reach speeds up to 35,000 RPM and fling tiny pieces of gel coat and fibers, damaging your eyes instantly.

Using masking or duct tape, tape around the spot to be repaired and leave an area of about two or three inches around the crack. The tape will help protect the surrounding area from getting scratched while you are sanding.

I have a cordless Dremel tool that I can use with a small grinding wheel to expand the cracks. A few of the shops I know use an air-powered small die grinder to remove excess material. Even a sharp razor knife might be of value to cut the edges of the crack or scratch. The goal is to bevel or shape the area into a "V" so the filler material can be applied completely into the crack and smoothed at the edges.

If you do not have a power grinder, you can always hand-sand the area before filling. If the crack is big enough, you can take a small piece of sandpaper and sand the edges of the crack or chip. Using 80-grit sandpaper, sand the edges of the crack at an angle (bevel). The smaller cracks or scratches still need to be made large enough to accept and bond with the filler material.

After sanding, clean the area one more time with acetone or thinner to remove any dust, dirt, or moisture. If necessary, use a small brush and acetone to get down into the crack. You do not want to have any dirt or dust left, or the filler might not stick. After cleaning, make sure that the underlying layers of material are completely dry before applying the filler material.

After you are done with the sanding and grinding, make sure to clean the area that you will be filling with a clean, lint-free cloth and acetone. Make sure that you clean all the way to the bottom of the scratch or crack. Any dust or dirt left in the crack will prevent the filler from bonding and cause a future chip at the same spot. A small paintbrush or even a toothpick can help clean the small crevices. Make sure the acetone is completely dry before filling the crack.

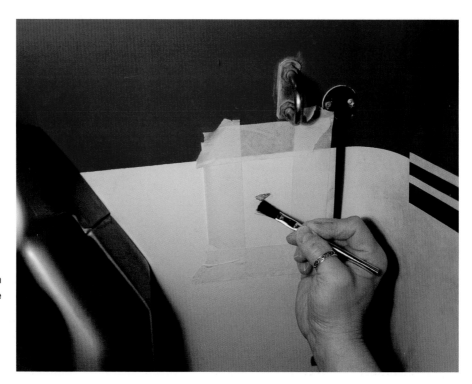

PROJECT 3 ★ *Filling*

When: Beginning and end of season

Time: 2–4 hours (drying time, 24 hours)

Tools: Sandpaper (320-, 400-, 600-, 800-, 1,200-grit); masking or duct tape; soft cloth; spreading paddle; bucket

Supplies: Acetone; gel-coat repair kit (or Maxi Repair Pack from West Systems); plastic body filler (Bondo); polyvinyl alcohol (PVA); household wax paper

Talent: ★★★

Tab: $15–75

Tip: If the gel coat is still tacky, clean the surface with a cloth and acetone. Do not overheat the filler or it will crack. Apply moderate heat to accelerate drying

Gain: Improved look, life of finish

For most small to medium repairs, if at all possible, try to fill the scratch with gel coat. Gel coat can act just like filler and will bond to the existing surface just as well as any other material, if the preparation is done correctly. Often a gel-coat repair does not have to be painted to match the rest of the surface, which helps to simplify the repair.

Using gel coats as the filler will also require that the gel-coat patch be coated with wax or sprayed with polyvinyl alcohol (PVA) so that the gel coat's surface will not be sticky. Originally the gel coat would be applied in a mold where the surface is treated with a wax or release agent. The wax allows the gel coat to dry completely, tack free. If the wax is not used, the surface of the gel coat will remain tacky or sticky. If the surface is sticky, there can't be any sanding or polishing.

One method for ensuring a fully cured gel-coat surface is to tape a sheet of wax paper over the patched area and allow the gel coat to dry. The wax paper should allow the gel coat to cure fully and not be sticky to the touch. You can also spray the gel coat with PVA after it has started to dry, but hasn't fully cured. Yet, that would mean having a small touchup paint gun and an air hose, an air compressor that requires electricity, and so on. Simple is better.

To keep it simple, some people just clean the dry gel-coat repair with a cloth and acetone. The acetone will help remove the sticky top surface of the gel coat after it has dried. Using a combination of the two methods is the best. Applying the wax paper and then cleaning with the acetone should eliminate the tacky surface.

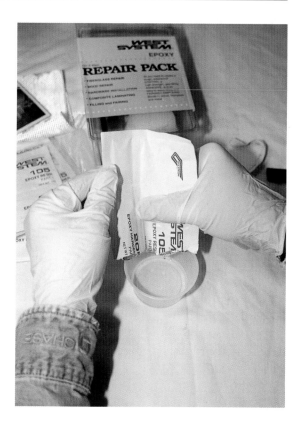

The West System Maxi Repair Pack comes with premeasured epoxy packets, fillers, mixing tools, and even gloves. All you need to do is tear open the containers, squeeze the epoxy and hardener into the provided cups, and stir with the enclosed mixing paddles.

21

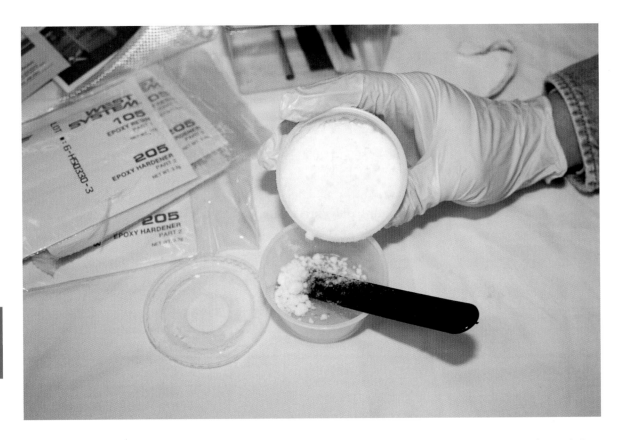

The epoxy was going to be used to fill a few small holes around the boat. One was a screw-in snap for the cockpit cover. The filler helps to thicken the epoxy so it can fill the small hole. You can use the epoxy and filler to fill cracks and build up small areas. Without the filler, the epoxy is too runny to hold any shape, but it can be used with cloth to cover a crack or reinforce an area.

Once the filler and epoxy have been thoroughly mixed (and in the right consistency), it's applied to the holes around the boat. A couple small pieces of masking tape were placed over the filled area to help keep the epoxy level with the surface of the boat. This hole will then be redrilled so that the replacement snap can be installed.

Spectrum provides color-matched gel-coat products for over 6,000 manufacturer's colors. The company offers a repair paste or gel coat by the quart. Whichever you use, mix it according to Spectrum's instructions and apply it with a spreading paddle, as smooth as possible. The smoother the finish after the gel coat has dried, the less sanding is needed.

Mix the gel coat as the manufacturer's directions indicate and apply to the scratch or crack. If it is a small surface scratch, apply the gel coat with a small disposable brush. If it is larger, use a small plastic spreading paddle.

After applying the gel coat, cover it with the wax paper or spray it with PVA.

Typically, gel coat needs thinning to be sprayed, but it is too thin for filling big cracks or holes. In that case, the gel coat needs to have a filler material (ground fiberglass) mixed in for thickening. If that isn't going to work, you can always use Bondo. Bondo is the brand name of a plastic filler that was designed for leveling surfaces and filling cracks and chips. Typically, the use of plastic filler will necessitate painting the area (with paint or thinned gel coat) when it is completed.

Reapply the masking or duct tape around the repair area. Leave about 3 inches of space to work in. This will again protect the surrounding area from damage.

Mix the filler (Bondo) according to the manufacturer's instructions. Do not attempt to add more hardener to accelerate the process. Increasing the drying time will only create cracks and bubbles that will require more filler. Mix the filler and apply with the plastic spreading paddle (available at the supply store where the filler was purchased). Most scratches or cracks will take at least two applications. Do not try applying one thick coat of filler. Start with a thin layer and wait for the material to dry. In between coats of filler, sand with 80-grit sandpaper and clean the area with acetone again. Then apply another thin layer of the filler.

You can warm the filler to accelerate the curing before the final sanding, but do not over heat. Just place it in the sun, set up a heat lamp, or use a hair dryer to speed up the drying time. The material needs to dry completely and change size (shrink) before sanding. If you sand the area before it is completely dried, it may shrink too much and the filler will need to be reapplied. Give it a chance to dry all the way through. Don't rush the drying too much by applying heat too close to the patch, or the filler will crack.

If you don't want to use Bondo, you can use epoxy resin with fillers to repair cracks. In that case, look into investing in one of West Systems' repair packs, available at most boating shops. I have the Maxi Repair Pack. Now for the sales pitch: The Maxi Repair Pack contains six 105 Resin/205 Hardener packets, a low-density filler for fairing, and a high-density filler for bonding. It also includes two application brushes, one syringe, two pipe cleaners, four mixing sticks, one pair of disposable gloves, four cleaning pads, mixing cups, and illustrated instructions.

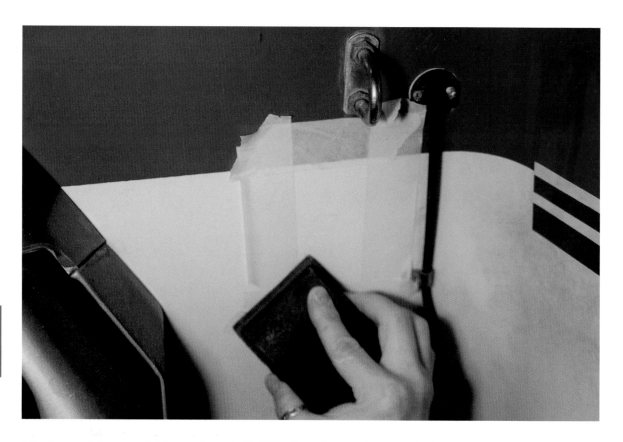

After the repair has completely cured, sand with 320-grit wet/dry sandpaper and a lot of freshwater. After the filled area is smooth and level, remove any surrounding tape and sand the same area, plus about 2 more inches around it, with 400-grit wet/dry sandpaper in preparation for the finish coat. If it was a small scratch, the area can be sanded with 600-grit wet/dry sandpaper and then polished with a quality rubbing compound. In that case, it might not even need to be painted.

To paint, after the filler is dry, sand the filler with a block sander fitted with 320-grit wet/dry sandpaper and a bucket of clean water. After the filled area is level and smooth, sand the repaired area using 400-grit wet/dry sandpaper and a lot of water. Make sure you use freshwater so the old, coarse sandpaper particles do not gouge the smooth surface.

Remove the tape. The surrounding area should be sanded smooth with 600-grit, wet/dry sandpaper and a clean bucket of water. Sand an area that is about 3 to 4 inches around the repaired area.

This is the area that will be painted with a matching color paint or gel coat. Sometimes you can get a manufacturer to provide a color-matched paint or gel coat. If you can't get the gel coat to match, you might be able to get an auto paint store to mix paint to match. Many manufacturers do not provide the color-matched gel coat for older boat models. Often they will refer you (or the shop) to a company like Spectrum Color to provide the gel coat. Check out what your local dealer can get before you start the project. Make sure you can get the correct colors and material.

PROJECT 4 ★ *Finishing*

When: Beginning and end of season

Time: 2–4 hours (drying time, 24 hours)

Tools: Sandpaper (250-, 400-, 600-, 800-, 1,200-grit); buffing compound; marine paste wax; masking tape; soft cloth; power buffer and pad (or cordless drill with buffing pad); paint gun and air compressor; bucket

Supplies: Acetone; color-matched paint or gel coat

Talent: ★★★

Tab: $15–75

Tip: The finer the grit, the more water needed to keep the sandpaper from clogging

Gain: Easier polishing and better, smoother finish

If you applied the gel coat as filler, all you might need to do is sand the filler gel coat down until the repair is smooth with the rest of the surface. If the colors are very close, a good polish might be able to blend the area together. Yet, more than likely, the repair will be visible even if it was filled with a color-matched gel coat. That will require applying a finish layer of paint or gel coat. The finish can be applied with a brush or with a spray gun. If you can buy the color-matched paint in an aerosol can, it can save you a lot of headaches. If not, you will need a small touchup paint gun, air compressor, and assorted hoses and fittings. The high-volume, low-pressure, gravity-feed paint guns are the easiest to use. They require very low air pressure, and they reduce the amount of overspray generated. Besides, they are pretty inexpensive. There are a few very nice touchup paint guns available for less than $30. Check out the auto supply or home improvement stores.

Today, gravity-free, high-volume, low-pressure (HVLP) paint guns can be purchased for less than $30. With a small compressor and a HVLP touchup gun, anyone can make the finish look like it was done by a professional. Whenever you are spray painting (gun or aerosol can), there is the risk of airborne chemicals being inhaled, or drifting and covering surrounding boats and equipment. Make sure you have taken all the necessary safety precautions to prevent any problems. When spraying paint or gel coat, follow the manufacturer's recommendations to get the right consistency for the finish. Use very light coats and keep the spray pattern at a 90-degree angle from the surface. The movement must be smooth and steady.

After the paint or gel coat is fully cured, you will need to polish the surface. It might need to be sanded first with a very fine sandpaper (800-grit wet/dry). Let the polisher do the work. Do not press too hard or stay in one place too long, and keep the polisher moving to prevent damage to the newly painted surface.

Tape the area with masking or duct tape before spraying. You will need a larger area to spray and blend the color. You will want to paint an area about 4 inches bigger than the repair. Also make sure you have sanded the area to be sprayed. Check that any trim, cleats, or fittings are either removed or taped for their protection from overspray. It will also be necessary to tape masking paper around the area to prevent the paint from drifting onto other parts of the boat. Buy an inexpensive drop cloth and cover the rest of the boat to prevent too much overspray.

Whether you are using paint or gel coat, you will want to apply a light coat of the color material over the repaired area and the rest of the sanded area to help blend the colors. Gel coat will usually only take one coat, but paint will probably take more than one coat.

You can brush the gel coat onto the area, but the gel coat is not self-leveling, meaning that it will only be as smooth as the application. Spraying will help with a smoother finish. But, if you do need to brush it on the surface, the brushstroke lines will need to be sanded after the material has cured completely. Using a high-quality natural bristle brush usually provides the best results.

After the gel coat has cured completely, start the sanding process in preparation for the polishing. If you applied a light coating of gel coat, you will need to clean the repaired area one last time with acetone to remove the tacky surface of the gel coat.

Wet sanding should be done with at least a 320- or 400-grit wet/dry sandpaper if you sprayed the material on. If you brushed on the gel coat, you will need to start with a 250-grit sandpaper to get the brush marks lowered and then sand with 400-grit sandpaper. Remember to use lots of water to help remove the material from the surface.

After sanding, dry the area completely with a soft, clean cloth and start polishing.

PROJECT 5 ★ *Polishing*

When: Beginning and end of season

Time: 4–8 hours, depending on size of boat

Tools: Bucket; hose and spray nozzle; sponge or wash mitt; chamois to remove water; dry towels; soft cloth; polish-applicator pad; power buffer and pad (or cordless drill with buffing pad)

Supplies: Buffing compound; mild dishwashing detergent; clean water

Talent: ★★

Tab: $25–100

Tip: Polishing on lift: Use cordless or polish by hand to prevent electrocution. Best to remove the boat from the water for access to all of the boat

Gain: Looks, life of surface, performance

Why clean the finish? Boats develop a buildup of oxidation from the water and the sun. The best way to protect the finish is to clean and polish it on a regular basis. Besides protecting the underlying fiberglass and gel coat, it will protect the trim and make it look better.

External polishing is a simple but time-consuming activity. The bigger the boat, the longer the polishing job takes. It can be done by hand, but now is a really good time to use that cordless drill and buffing pad. The easiest way to complete the process is to have the boat out of the water and on a trailer or stands. If

There are many different opinions about how to apply the polish. Many auto finish shops apply the polish to the polishing pad and then spread it on the surface to be polished. A few shops put the polish onto the surface first. I like to apply a coat of the polish with an applicator pad or clean cloth. It gives me an opportunity to see the surface I am polishing and to make sure I get an even coat of the polish applied.

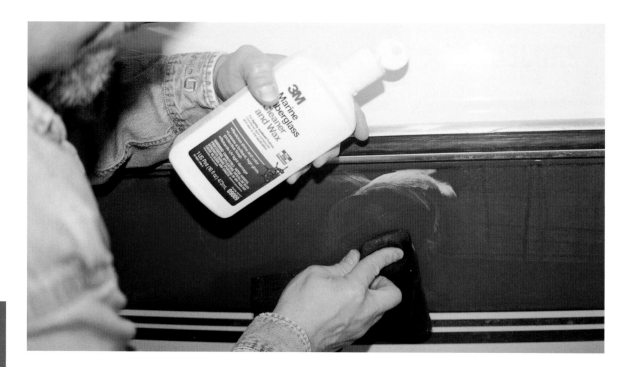

3M makes a one-step cleaner and wax that works very well. If you decide to apply it with a clean cloth, rub the cleaner into the surface until the cleaner's color has started to disappear. Then you either start to polish with a clean cloth and a lot of elbow grease or . . .

the finish is not very dirty, scratched, or oxidized, I'd jump right into the waxing. If it needs cleaning and polishing, start there.

Never start waxing or polishing the external fiberglass finish until you have washed the surface with a mild detergent and water. Any dirt or sand that might be on the finish will be ground into the surface and create more problems then you ever expected. So first, give the boat a bath.

Also, whenever you are using a polisher—it doesn't matter if it is a big, two-handed professional model or the cordless drill variety—make sure you never press down or put any weight on the buffer. Just let the buffer weight do all the work. This is a little difficult on vertical surfaces, but as you start buffing, you will be able to tell if you are pressing the buffer into the finish. The idea is that if you put too much pressure on the buffing pad, you will probably burn the finish. Also, don't stay in one area for any length of time. Go over the surface as needed.

First, you must understand that a heavily oxidized finish or an algae buildup on the hull will require a little extra work to clean. This is a job that should be done *before* you polish and wax the boat. There are specialized cleaners available, if necessary, but most are very caustic, can be hazardous, and are

not environmentally friendly. If possible, clean the boat with a good fiberglass cleaner available from most marine supply stores.

Apply the cleaner with a disposable brush to the algae-covered area. Use rubber gloves and eye protection while working with the cleaner. Follow the manufacturer's instructions and scrape the area with a plastic scraper to remove the algae. Repeat the process until the algae is removed.

Different people have different methods for applying the polishing compound. Some people feel that you should apply the compound directly to the pad and swirl it around the surface before you turn on the buffer. Others apply the compound with a separate pad to the surface first.

Be very careful around the trim and edges. If painted, this is the place the paint is going to be the thinnest. If gel-coated, this is the area that is at risk of burning. Always try to use a new buffer pad, especially on new paint. An old pad could damage the paint from the contaminants left over in the pad's fiber. Always keep an eye out for (and avoid) the buffer's cord and the boat's antennas.

After the boat is cleaned and dried off, start polishing from the top. Before climbing on the deck, make sure that you are not wearing clothing or shoes

. . . you use a clean buffing pad attached to your cordless drill or a power buffer. If you are buffing near graphics, mask them off to make sure that you do not tear or damage the graphics with the power buffer. If you are buffing a painted surface, do not let the buffer stay in one place for any length of time or it will burn the paint (or any finish, for that matter).

that have hard metal or plastic parts that can scratch the finish. You might even want to kneel on a "gardening" foam pad or a clean towel to pad your knees and protect the surface.

You have two options for polishing and waxing the boat. You can polish with a polishing compound and then wax using a separate paste wax, or you can use one of the combination polish/waxes. If your boat is in need of serious cleaning, you'll probably want to opt for the separate processes for the first major cleaning. If it were not too heavily oxidized, I would start with the multipurpose products. The multipurpose products sold by StarBrite, 3M, and Blue Coral offer a one-step polish and wax. All you will need to do is apply the liquid and buff the area—it's done. A multipurpose product sure simplifies the process, although a good coat of paste wax on the topside would still help protect the deck's finish.

Start on the topside (deck) with whatever product you are using. Using the top-down method ensures you are not climbing on or dragging cords over the areas you have already polished. Work from the center out.

Apply the polishing compound with a clean cloth or polish applicator over a small, manageable area. Typically, about two square feet will be enough. After it is applied, buff the surface with the power buffer. Moving the buffer in a circular pattern helps to keep the buffing pad from wearing in one particular spot. Remember, don't linger in any one area or you may burn the finish. Besides keeping the buffer moving, it is important to keep the pad from getting clogged with polish. Don't put too much polish on the finish. It only takes a very light coat to buff the finish to a shine.

Keep clean polishing pads available because the pads will get clogged with paint, oils, and wax. Clean the dirty pads with soap and water; then let them dry completely.

Again, this is a simple but time-consuming job. After the deck is completed, move to the sides of the hull and work your way around the boat at the same level. After you have buffed the sides, work your way to the bottom. An automotive-style "creeper" can come in handy if you are located on a smooth surface where it can roll under the boat and trailer. If not, an old piece of carpet can be used as a pad to lie on while buffing the bottom areas. If the boat is on a trailer, it will not be possible to buff all the areas; rollers or pads will block some spots. Remember to wear eye protection.

PROJECT 6 ★ *Waxing*

When: Beginning and end of season

Time: 4–8 hours, depending on size of boat

Tools: Soft cloth; wax-applicator pad; power buffer and pad (or cordless drill with buffing pad); soft-bristle toothbrush

Supplies: Marine paste wax

Talent: ★

Tab: $7–10

Tip: Polishing on lift: Use cordless or polish by hand to avoid electrocution. It's best to remove the boat from the water to access as much of the boat as possible

Gain: More difficult for oxidation and dirt to stick to finish

After the boat is completely polished, it's time to add a coat of a quality marine paste wax (carnauba is the best). Why wax? Waxing is a major part of the exterior care process. The top surfaces of the vessel (the deck, hatches, etc.) should be the minimum area waxed. This wax coating will help protect these top surfaces from sun damage. Of course, it will also protect the finish from the other elements that a boat encounters, such as hard water and algae.

Like polishing, waxing should be done in small areas. A good carnuba-based paste wax should be applied by hand and allowed to dry to a white powder look before buffing.

Power buffing of the wax can speed up the process and make the surface shine. It can also damage the paint or finish if you get careless and don't clean the buffing pad, put too much pressure on the buffer, or linger too long in one spot.

Areas around cleats or fittings may need to be cleaned with a soft toothbrush. If possible, clean with a cloth, but if that doesn't get that last little bit of wax, use the toothbrush to finish the job.

Of course, if you used a combination polish/wax you could skip this step. But it doesn't hurt to wax the complete boat with a quality paste wax. Waxing should be done at least once a year, minimum. But twice a year is better, usually in the fall and spring. At least be sure to get a coat on the top surfaces. The wax should be applied to small sections of the boat. Do not wax too large an area at one time. If you tackle small sections it makes the job easier, and you seem to get better results. Don't put the wax on in direct sunlight. Often the sun can dry the wax before it can be rubbed into the paint.

The removal of the wax can be done by hand or with a power buffer. If you use a power buffer, it's the same idea as polishing. Use a clean buffing pad and do not put any pressure on the buffer. There are lots of different types of specialized buffer/wax machines available, but you can use the cordless drill with a soft waxing pad to do the job.

There are benefits to waxing your boat by hand. Besides building the arm muscles, it gives the person waxing an opportunity to look over the finish, fittings, and trim. It's a good time for that final view of the boat's exterior. This is also a time to make sure all the cleats are firmly attached, and they can also get a coat of wax. The wood items on the boat should be inspected to ensure that they are sealed and protected from moisture damage.

PROJECT 7 ★ *Wood Repair and Sealing*

When: Beginning and end of season

Time: 3–5 hours (drying time, 24 or more hours)

Tools: Sandpaper (320-, 600-grit); gallon bucket; stiff-bristled scrub brush; cordless Dremel tool; sanding drum bit

Supplies: Wood cleaner (specialized, dependent on type of wood); liquid electric dishwashing detergent; wood oil or sealer (dependent on the type of wood)

Talent: ★ ★ ★

Tab: $25–45

Tip: Dishwashing detergent helps remove stains from the wood. Sand with the grain

Gain: More difficult for oxidation and dirt to stick to finish

Where's the wood? Most of the boats we are working with are not using wood as visible major component in the construction, but as trim or accessory pieces. Items such as boarding ladders, swim platforms, steps, or surface protectors typically are constructed with teakwood. Teakwood is also used as a flooring material. There are a couple of maintenance items that need to be performed on

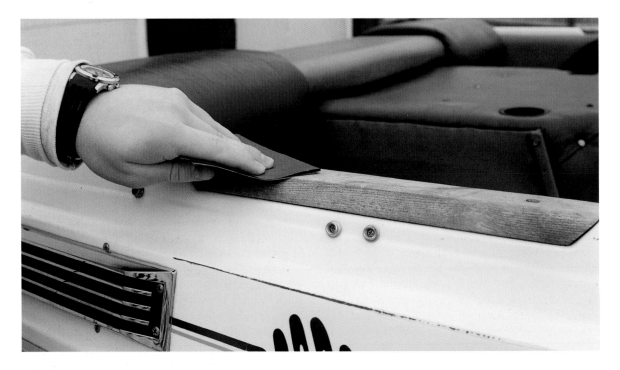

Most wood can be sanded with a 400- to 600-grit wet/dry sandpaper. The best thing to do is to sand the wood with dry sandpaper and then moisten the wood with water to see if any of the sanded fibers stick up. After the wood dries, sand it again to remove those standing fibers. Tape the area around the wood so that you do not sand the fiberglass. In this case, you are preparing the boat for painting anyway.

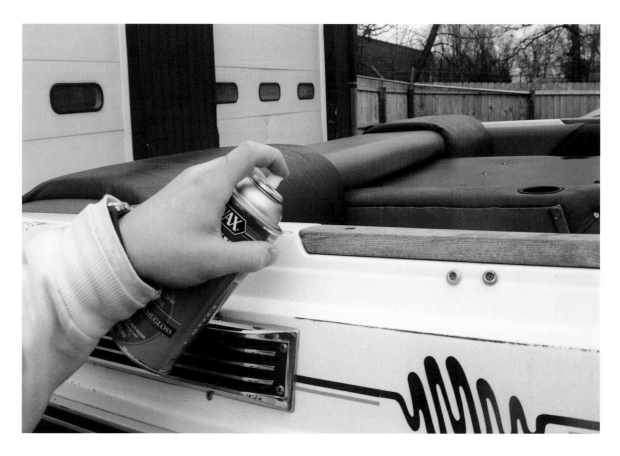

Wood can be oiled, sealed, or coated. Most of the local mechanics choose to spray the wood with a polyurethane finish. They feel it lasts longer and requires less care in the future.

the wood. The wood needs to be cleaned and it needs to be protected. There are numerous wood cleaners available. All have their advantages and disadvantages. For some stubborn stains it may be necessary for the wood to be cleaned by these specialized cleaners. However, for general cleaning you can use electric dishwasher detergent. Lightly scrub the stained area with a soft but stiff brush, and rinse with lots of water.

If the wood is soft or develops cracks, it will lose its strength. Cracks and splinters make the wood a safety hazard. That means it needs to be replaced or repaired. If the wood is cracked, it should be replaced. If the wood is soft and flexes as a step, it should be replaced. If it is soft and is a deck step, not wholly supporting any weight, it can be left alone.

If the wood is splintering, chipping, or cracking on the edges, remove the broken part or splinter and sand the area with sandpaper. The sharp edge can be sanded with 320-grit paper and oiled or varnished,

depending on how it was finished originally. When possible, always try to sand with the grain.

Feeling tired? Using the Dremel cordless tool with a small-drum sanding attachment can really speed up the repair time. Sand the crack or chip with the Dremel.

After the wood is dry from the cleaning or sanding, wet the wood with water. Let the wood dry. Water will make the loose wood fibers stand up. After the wood has dried, re-sand with fine sandpaper. This will make for a little smoother finish.

Apply the appropriate oil to the wood with a disposable paintbrush or a cloth. The oil should be rubbed into the wood and allowed to dry. Any excess oil should be wiped off with a clean, dry cloth.

A number of shops in our area actually stain the wood and give it a coat of clear polyurethane sealer. They feel this will last longer and requires less maintenance in the future compared to just staining and oiling the wood.

PROJECT 8 ★ *Cleaning Fittings*

When: Each time you take the boat out

Time: 1–2 hours

Tools: Dremel cordless tool and carbon steel or stainless brush set; hard plastic kitchen scrapers; toothbrush or small stiff-bristle brush

Supplies: Cola; metal polish/cleaner; aerosol cooking oil; ice and glass for drinks

Talent: ★★

Tab: $25

Tip: Deep corrosion may require harsher chemical cleaners or replacement

Gain: Reduces fiberglass stains from corrosion on metal fittings

Most of the fittings on a boat are stainless chrome or aluminum. Many of the fittings will start corroding after exposure to the elements over time. If the corrosion is serious enough, replacement might be the only option. But if the corrosion has not ruined the fitting, but just the looks, you can often clean the fittings.

The first step is trying to get rid of the corrosion. Try cleaning by using a hard plastic scraper (like you would find in a kitchen supply store) and remove as much of the external corrosion as possible. If the scraper doesn't do the job, get out the Dremel cordless tool and a small wire brush.

There are different wire brushes available for different materials. Dremel's literature states, "Stainless steel brushes do not cause 'after-rust' when used on corrosive-resistant materials like pewter, aluminum, and stainless steel. Carbon steel brushes are versatile brushes for removing rust and corrosion, polishing metal surfaces, de-burring and blending surface junctures, and cleaning electrical components. And brass brushes are non-sparking and softer than steel. They will not scratch soft metals like gold, copper, brass." The assortment can be great, and actually overwhelming. So, if you stick with the carbon steel or stainless steel brushes, you should be able to remove almost any corrosion buildup on the fittings.

The Dremel tool works wonders on spots of corrosion. There are numerous types of wire brushes available that can remove the rust, oxidation, and corrosion from all types of fittings. Their small size allows the brush to get in areas of the fitting. Carbon steel brushes are probably the most versatile to have in your tool kit. Brushes will remove the corrosion and oxidation from most of the fittings without damaging the fitting. There are also brushes that are made specifically for brass and stainless steel.

The next step is to apply metal cleaner and polish. Most cleaners and polishes are a liquid format that is applied to the metal, rubbed in, and wiped off. There are different products for different materials. Certain chemicals should not be used on aluminum, but can be used on brass or stainless. Read the manufacturer's instructions carefully when applying compounds to your fittings, trim pieces, and railings. Of course, I also like the Dremel polishing bits for this job. A polishing pad spinning at thousands of RPMs can make a chrome or stainless part really glisten.

A carbonated can of cola is a simple and cheaper cleaner. That's right, buy a generic version of cola (or you can use the expensive version, Coca-Cola) at the local grocery store, pour it on the fittings, and scrub them with a stiff bristled brush. While this is not going to be as effective as a commercial cleaner, it is less caustic and environmentally friendly. This will take care of most of the minor surface corrosion that you find on fittings, cleats, or even parts of the outboard or stern drive units. Personally, I haven't had really good luck with this. It does take off some of the corrosion, but I like a quality metal polish. I usually put the cola in a glass with ice and drink it instead.

After cleaning, spray a light coating of an aerosol cooking oil (like PAM) on the fittings. This coating helps prevent acids from sticking to the fixtures, thereby reducing the risk of future corrosion. Remember: This just reduces the risk, it doesn't eliminate it. The fittings will need to be continually cleaned and protected to keep from being damaged. This is one of those ongoing care items.

I've used Mother's Polish since my Harley days. It has always been able to clean and shine any kind of metal I have used it on. Apply a liberal amount and rub it into the surface with a clean cloth until the metal shines. Clean the excess off with another clean cloth.

The Dremel comes through again. Dremel offers a small buffing disc that can be used to shine areas where your fingers won't reach. The mandrel that holds the disc has a screw tip. You screw the felt disc onto it, and that sometimes leaves the point of the mandrel sticking past the disc. Be careful not to scratch the finish of the fitting or the boat with the sharp tip of the mandrel.

PROJECT 9 ★ *Nonskid Surface Care*

When: Beginning and end of season

Time: 1 hour

Tools: Scrub brush; gallon bucket

Supplies: Nonskid deck cleaner or liquid dishwashing soap

Talent: ★

Tab: $5–10

Tip: Do not use cloth to clean; the texture of the nonskid surface can tear fibers from the cloth. To dry the area, blot it dry, don't rub

Gain: Better footing, safety

It doesn't matter if the nonskid flooring is an adhesive stick-on, painted on, or part of the gel-coat finish; cleaning it is the easiest way to extend its life. Most of the stick-on material I find is located on the trailer or lift, and only occasionally on a boat's surface. Most of today's boats have the nonskid incorporated right into the finish.

There are dedicated cleaners such as the nonskid deck cleaner from StarBrite, or you can use a mild liquid soap mixed with water and brushed on the nonskid area with a medium stiff-bristled scrub brush. If you use a grease-cutting detergent, make sure that all the residue is rinsed from the area and diluted with water. If not, the chemicals could actually etch or damage the gel-coat finish.

If your nonskid surface isn't preventing skidding very well, there are a couple of ways to fix it. You can always paint a new surface. That requires cleaning and priming the existing surface, and then painting the surface with an epoxy paint that has the nonskid material mixed into the paint, or painting the surface and sprinkling the nonskid material on the wet paint.

If the nonskid material is adhesive back (stick-on), all you have to do is remove the old and replace it with new. Most of the adhesive-back nonskid that I've seen recently has been on trailer step pads, and not on boat decks. Although there are a number of older boats that used adhesive nonskid as original equipment, and many owners who have added it at a later time, it isn't the most common today.

The first thing to do is to remove the existing material. Although this sounds like an easy task, it can be very difficult. A stiff plastic paint scraper or a plastic kitchen scraper can be used to get between the nonskid material and the surface. A razor-blade scraper can be used, but there is a higher risk of scratching and gouging the underlying material.

Once a corner or edge is lifted, grasp the material by hand or with a small pair of pliers. As you pull the

StarBrite has a number of different boat-cleaning chemicals, one of which is designed specifically for nonskid surfaces. Use it directly from the container or use a mild liquid soap and water. Stay away from dishwashing machine liquid soap. It can damage the finish of the gel coat if it is not completely rinsed from the surface.

The nonskid cleaner or soap needs to be brushed over the rough nonskid surface with a medium stiff-bristle brush. The brush needs to be stiff enough to clean the surface, but not so stiff that it will scratch the finish of the gel coat.

material back at a 180-degree angle, scrape along the folded line and the deck. Folding it back on itself helps to prevent the material from tearing and breaking away. Pull the material slow and steady.

Sometimes a chemical adhesive remover or solvent like Goo Gone, or even acetone, should be applied as the material is being pulled up. If you apply a little of the remover along the edge, it will break down the adhesive, and the scraper will help to push it under the edge that is still attached. Too much acetone or adhesive remover could soften the scraper, so use it sparingly.

After the original stick-on nonskid is removed, remove the adhesive with a cleaner like Goo Gone. Now that the adhesive is removed, clean the area with solvent like acetone to remove any of the remaining adhesive, oils, or chemicals.

Cut the replacement nonskid material to the correct size and shape, remove the backing, and starting at one end, carefully roll the material onto the surface. Make sure there are not any wrinkles or air bubbles.

After the material is removed, use a solvent like Goo Gone to remove the adhesive from the surface. After the adhesive has been removed, you will need to clean the area with acetone or paint thinner to remove any oil or solvent. Once clean and dry, you can sand the area with a 320-grit sandpaper. After sanding, again clean with acetone or thinner before installing the replacement nonskid material.

When removing adhesive-backed, nonskid material, you might need a razor knife to scrape under the edges. Grip the material and pull it directly away from the surface with a slow and steady pressure.

INTERIOR
Projects 10 through 12

The interior of your boat will be subject to wet swimsuits, damp breezes, and stale air, not to mention spilled food and drink, so keeping the fabric clean and fresh can make the material last longer and keep the boating experience pleasant.

Your best defense for the resulting stains and odors is cleaning the interior on a regular basis. In addition, using a fabric or vinyl treatment extends the life of the material and makes the cooped-up boating experience more enjoyable.

Also, any material that is exposed to the sun needs to be protected from drying, cracking, and fading. The materials used in the seats, cushions, trim, and floor covering need to be cleaned and treated to protect them from the harmful rays of the sun and damaging humidity.

Interior care should be an ongoing process throughout the boating season.

Most cabin areas get very little wear and tear. *Bill Fedorko*

PROJECT 10 ★ *Upholstery Care*

When: Each time you take the boat out

Time: 1–2 hours

Tools: Fabric scrub brush; vacuum; gallon bucket

Supplies: Fabric cleaner; mild clothing detergent; household white vinegar; spray Scotch Guard; vinyl cleaner and conditioner; fabric glue; vinyl repair kit

Talent: ★★

Tab: $2–10

Tip: Test the cleaner on the vinyl or fabric in a small and inconspicuous area to make sure it doesn't fade colors. Try fabric glue and a patch first, then use thread as backup. If the cover can be removed and you have access to a sewing machine, zigzag stitching is the best method of repair

Gain: Maintains boat's value, extends lifespan and boating experience

Keeping the upholstery clean and protected will help maintain its looks, it will last longer, and, in turn, enhance the boat's resale value. Patching the material when it gets small tears and rips can prolong the life span of the fabric. Dirty material and tears in the upholstery also reduce the resale value of the boat.

Typical boat interiors are made of a vinyl material that is designed to withstand water and sun, but it doesn't last forever. Interior upholstery needs to be

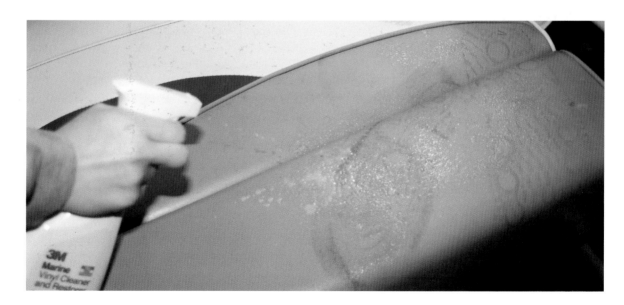

Vinyl is the most popular material for boat interiors (outside the cabin areas). Vinyl can be cleaned with a mixture of mild soap and water, or a dedicated vinyl cleaner. 3M's vinyl cleaner not only cleans, but it also conditions the material. The boat's interior is susceptible to UV rays and harsh weather conditions, so it needs to have some form of protection. Numerous companies make specialized conditioners and cleaners; they are available at marine stores or local auto departments of major discount stores.

Scrub the soap or cleaner into the stains with a soft-bristle brush.

cleaned and treated on a regular basis to extend its life for as long as possible.

Removing stains from vinyl materials can be done with water, a mild clothing detergent, and a little vinegar. You can also use spray upholstery cleaner or a spray vinyl cleaner, which are available from discount, marine, or auto supply stores. Whichever you use, after cleaning, the vinyl should be treated with a vinyl conditioner to keep it from drying out and becoming brittle. Dry, brittle vinyl will crack and chip, become uncomfortable, and eventually be damaged beyond repair.

A quality vinyl conditioner should be used after each boating excursion. 3M makes a vinyl cleaner and conditioner that reduces the number of steps in the process. Spray it on the vinyl, scrub the stains, and wipe it off; the vinyl is cleaned and treated in one step. If you happen to have leather on your boat (not many do), make sure you use quality leather cleaner and conditioner to keep the leather supple and clean.

Fabric is usually used only on the cabin cushions. You don't see many fabric seats in the cockpits of boats. They soak up the moisture, mildew, and mold, and also deteriorate from the sun so rapidly that they

are not cost-effective. Yet, they are used in the cabin areas that are not as susceptible to moisture and sunlight, and they do need to be cleaned and maintained.

Cleaning your interior fabrics (seats, trim, pads) is no different than cleaning the sofa at home. You will need to test a sample of the fabric or vinyl cleaner on a small area to make sure it is color-safe, and then start applying it to the material with a soft cloth. Hard-to-remove stains may need additional treatment, or the use of an additional stain remover.

Typically, fabric cleaner is sprayed on the fabric, allowed to dry, and then fabric is vacuumed after the cleaner dries. Any household upholstery cleaner can be used. Most of the newer marine fabrics are mold- and mildew-resistant, but a little extra cleaning and a light treatment of Scotch Guard can keep the moisture absorption to a minimum.

If you need to make any repairs, think of them as a stopgap measure. Most upholstery shops do not recommend patches or vinyl repair kits as a long-term solution. Due to a boat's sun and water exposure, they recommend having the damaged area completely replaced. But, there are vinyl and fabric repair kits available that will allow you to patch the

Many of the vinyl glues actually "melt" the materials together, so it is important not to put very much of the glue on the surrounding area of the tear. Apply a small drop from the tube, or use a toothpick or cotton swab to apply the glue in and under the tear. Tape or clamp the material in place until it has cured (dried). Clean the surrounding area of excess glue with a paper towel or cotton swab.

tear and apply a material that is supposed to make the tear or hole look like new. I've never had the greatest luck with this patch by itself. Usually I patch the tear or hole with glue and maybe a small piece of fabric. Often this will last until the end of the season, or until I have time to have the repair done by an upholstery shop. Small tears or punctures have lasted as long as I've owned the boat.

If you do want to make a repair, start with a small piece of material and a tube of fabric glue (or even Superglue). Fabric glue is available from most craft or sewing stores (including Wal-Mart).

Not all repairs will need a piece of fabric, but if there is a hole that needs to be patched, you will want to put a small reinforcement under the tear. Any similar fabric will do to add the strength, but if you look for a little extra fabric on the inside of the cushion or under the seats, the match will be better. Often there will be enough leftover material under the seat or on a seam inside the cushion to cut a patch.

Cut a small patch from the leftover material that is just a little bigger than the tear. If you are patching a zippered cushion, you should be able to remove the stuffing material and turn the cover inside out. This would allow you to glue the fabric patch directly over the tear and let it cure, possibly with a weight on the area. If the patch is in an area that you can't get to the backside, you'll need to insert the patch material through the tear, insert the nozzle of the glue around the edges of the tear, and patch it.

In this case, a little stitching can help hold the patch in place. If you're really good with a needle and thread, you might not even need the glue (I like both, because I'm lousy with a needle and thread). A curved needle is a requirement when working on a tear from one side. You'll want to make small, looped stitches around the edge of the patch and even through the tear. The thread needs to be knotted on the underside of the tear so that it does not show from the top.

Once the glue has cured and the stitching is done, spray the area with a fabric protector like Scotch Guard.

In the case of a very small tear in the material, you can glue the area carefully with just the glue. Fill the tear with glue and remove any excess with a small cloth or cotton swab.

PROJECT 11 ★ *Carpet Care*

When: Each time you take the boat out, or at least the beginning and end of season

Time: 1–2 hours

Tools: Wet/dry vacuum; carpet scrub brush

Supplies: Spray carpet cleaner; household baking soda; no-damp moisture-absorption packets

Talent: ★

Tab: $15–25

Tip: Remember to vacuum before cleaning. Follow the manufacturer's instructions for the cleaner you are using

Gain: Comfort and longer life of the carpet

Cleaning carpets is not the most exciting maintenance job for a boat owner. It is still a very important process to extend the life of your boat. Most carpet manufacturers will tell you that the worst thing for carpets is the dirt and sand embedded in it. The granules grind and wear away at the carpet fibers and the backing material. Then, add a little moisture and you not only have damaged carpet

Vacuuming the stained area will remove the dirt before you apply the cleaner. You do not want to scrub the area and rub the dirt any further into the fibers than necessary. You should use a good wet/dry Shop Vac to ensure that any moisture will be removed with the dirt.

To avoid surprises, follow the manufacturer's instructions for applying the cleaning solution. Test a small area prior to spraying the cleaner in a visible area. Apply to the stain as directed.

fibers, but now your carpet can grow mold and mildew. Cleaning it regularly is not only recommended, but a necessary maintenance item.

Boats come with carpets that are glued or snapped onto the floor. If the carpets are snap-in or removable, take them out and place on the dock, concrete, or other level hard surface. Use a quality wet/dry vacuum to remove any sand and dirt.

After vacuuming the removed carpets, apply a household carpet cleaner to any stains. Per the manufacturer's instructions, you should always treat a small test area first to eliminate the risk of discoloration. Every now and then, a carpet dye can react with the cleaner and leave a spot that is a different color than the rest of the carpet.

After the cleaner is applied, follow the manufacturer's instructions. Typically you will spray the area, scrub with a stiff-bristle brush, and let it dry. Sometimes you will have to rinse the area with clean water and then let the area dry. Often the cleaner will re-

quire that you blot the area with a dry cloth or paper towels to remove any excess moisture. Depending on the cleaner you use, you might need to vacuum the area after it is dry. I used Woolite Oxy Deep Carpet Cleaner that required scrubbing the area with a brush, then vacuuming the moisture and stain away.

After the carpet is dry, you can sprinkle a light coating of baking soda over the carpet and brush it into the fibers with a stiff, bristled floor-cleaning brush. The carpet has to be dry before you apply the baking soda or you will create a pasty mess. Baking soda is well known as an odor-absorbing material. Sprinkling it in the carpet and rubbing it into the fibers will help remove unwanted odors from the carpet. You'll need to vacuum again to remove any of the remaining baking soda.

If you are not able to remove the carpets, you need to treat them the same way but do it in their location. It is very important to use a quality wet/dry Shop Vac to help remove any moisture that might be

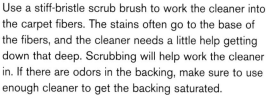
Use a stiff-bristle scrub brush to work the cleaner into the carpet fibers. The stains often go to the base of the fibers, and the cleaner needs a little help getting down that deep. Scrubbing will help work the cleaner in. If there are odors in the backing, make sure to use enough cleaner to get the backing saturated.

Vacuum with your wet/dry Shop Vac and remove the stain, dirt, and moisture. It takes quite a bit of power to pull the dirt and cleaner from deep in the fibers and the backing of the carpet. This is where a good Shop Vac is worth the money. After vacuuming, let the area dry completely. A small fan can help speed the drying process.

in the backing and fibers. Any moisture or dirt that remains in the carpet could affect the cleaner's final result.

After the carpets are clean, make sure the carpet dries completely. Because snap-in carpets can be removed, they get air on both sides to speed up the drying process. Permanently installed carpets dry from one side only (the top) and can take a long time. When you do cleaning that requires applying a chemical, it is recommended that this not be done in direct sunlight. The sunlight can heat

the chemicals and disrupt the cleaning process or dry the chemical prematurely.

An additional tip is to place "no-damp" moisture absorption packets in the boat when not it is not in use. Place them in enclosed lockers, compartments or cabinets, and around the cockpit area. This will help keep the humidity level down, alleviating some of the damp smells that will build in the carpet and fabrics. An alternative to the commercial no-damp packet is to use open boxes of baking soda placed throughout the boat.

PROJECT 12 ★ *Windshield Care*

When: Each time you take the boat out, or at least the beginning and end of season

Time: 1–2 hours

Tools: Fine wet/dry sandpaper; bucket; soft-bristle toothbrush; clean, soft cloth; sandpaper or emery cloth (320- to 400-grit wet/dry); masking tape (or duct tape); cordless Dremel tool; aluminum sanding and grinding bits

Supplies: Acrylic-glass cleaner and polish; dishwashing detergent; acrylic-friendly solvent (Goo Gone); aluminum polish

Talent: ★ ★ ★

Tab: $25–35

Tip: Acrylic scratches very easily. Do not use anything but approved cleaner. Bends or dents in the frame don't have to be perfect. Straighten and smooth them as best as possible. Only file if sharp edges or gouges are present

Gain: Better visibility

Boat manufacturers use tempered glass or acrylic plastic materials for the windshield. If the glass is nicked or chipped, you'll need to contact a glass-repair company to fix the damaged area (or replace it). There are glass-repair kits available in the auto section of most stores, so you could attempt try the repair yourself. Keep in mind, tempered glass is pretty difficult to work with using the normal repair

Rub the aluminum polish firmly on the aluminum frame. The polish will remove minor scratches from the finish. The frame will need to be cleaned with a dry, clean cloth to remove the dark residue from the aluminum and the polish. Nicks or deep scratches may need to be sanded or ground with the cordless Dremel tool prior to polishing. You can also use the Dremel for polishing, but by hand seems to work just as well.

Cleaning a windshield made from tempered glass is just like cleaning the windows at home or in your car. Spray a household glass cleaner like Windex on the glass, and then scrub the dirt and bugs away. Dry the windshield with a clean cloth and you are done. Sort of.

kits and polishing compounds. It's really best to leave repairs to a glass company and just worry about the cleaning. You can clean the glass with a dishwashing detergent (spot-free) and water, an automotive glass cleaner, or a household cleaner like Windex.

If the windshield is made from acrylic plastic, it's time to get out the acrylic polish and scratch remover. Deep scratches may need to be sanded with a very fine wet/dry sandpaper (800- to 1200-grit), but this is a *last* resort. It's usually best to just apply a polish/scratch remover.

Tempered glass is very difficult to sand. Also, there are disadvantages to sanding and polishing in one small area in the windshield. The sanding and buffing can actually change the level of the material, and distort the view when looking through the repaired location. Be careful not to sand and buff too much in a concentrated area.

Apply a liberal amount of plastic windshield polish, buff the area by hand or with a power buffer to remove any minor scratches, and polish the windshield. Polishing the windshield by

hand reduces the risk of burning the acrylic or distorting the area.

Clean the acrylic windshield with dishwashing soap and warm water, or a specialized acrylic cleaner. Use a very soft cloth and lots of water. Do not use paper towels or newspaper on acrylic because it will scratch the surface. If there is grease, oil, or tar on the acrylic, it can usually be removed with a soft cloth and solvent such as Goo Gone. You do need to make sure that the cleaner you use will not damage acrylic. Make sure you read the directions and warning labels before using any chemicals on acrylic. Also test a small amount on an out-of-the-way section of the windshield.

After polishing the glass, it's best to apply a coating of water repellent like Rain-X, or even a coat of a paste wax. Use a soft-bristled toothbrush to clean the wax from around the edges of the frame and glass. Do not apply wax to an acrylic windshield; stick to acrylic-specific products.

The glass is held in place by an aluminum or stainless-steel frame. Stress caused by bends or damage to the frames can cause breaking or cracking of

46

the glass or plastic. Damaged areas can have sharp edges or gouges that could leave sharp protruding pieces of metal to snag clothing and skin.

If the frame has serious bends, it is best to replace the damaged section of the frame or (if necessary) the complete windshield. Most bends are small areas that have been impacted by something (like that low tree branch from parking the boat next to the garage) that has collapsed the frame material and probably can't be removed. If there has been an impact that scraped the frame, leaving sharp edges, all you need to do is sand the area with a piece of fine sandpaper (320- to 400-grit wet/dry works great) or emery paper. If there is a large gouge, it might be necessary to file the area using a fine aluminum file, and then sand the area with sandpaper or emery cloth. Don't forget to apply masking tape (or duct tape) to the glass near the damaged frame so that the glass doesn't get sanded. Duct tape is a very good protector.

And you guessed it; you can use that cordless Dremel tool with a small sanding or grinding bit to remove nicks and scratches. Be careful any time you are using a power tool on aluminum, near the glass, or near plastic. One slip, and you can make a big gouge out of a small one. Sometimes sanding by hand can be safer.

After sanding, it's best to apply an aluminum polish to clean and shine the area.

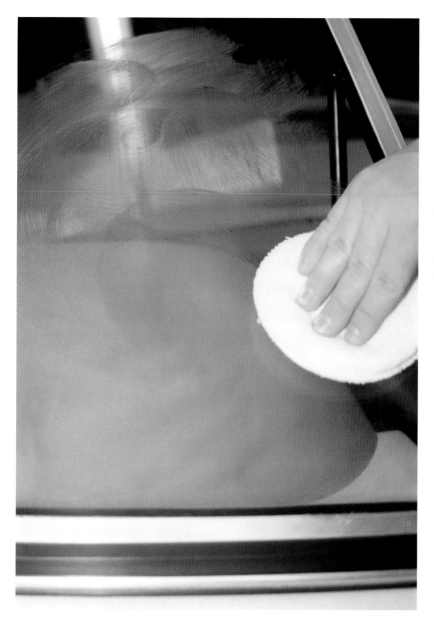

You need to apply a coat of paste wax or treat the windshield with a water-spot remover (like Rain-X) before going back on the lake. You can wash the windshield with a spot-free dishwashing liquid as an option. Apply the wax with a soft-applicator pad or cloth. Do not use anything abrasive on the glass. After the wax dries, use a soft cloth to remove the wax. If the windshield is acrylic, *do not* use anything that is not designed for acrylic windshields. Otherwise, serious damage can result.

SECTION 3

ENGINE
Projects 13 through 21

The largest population of boats are the ones with outboard motors installed. The National Marine Manufacturers Association (NMMA) estimates that more than 212,000 outboard boats were sold in 2002. The NMMA also estimates that more than 69,300 stern-drive boats and over 22,300 inboard boats were purchased in 2002.

Depending on your boat, inboard engines can be mounted below the floor, in the middle of the boat, or at the transom. Whatever the installation, the basics are all the same. There is an internal combustion engine with a fuel system, electrical system, cooling system, and drive system. Whether it's diesel or gas, two-stroke cycle or four-stroke, it doesn't really matter. There are things that an owner can do to help reduce wear and tear and extend the lifespan.

Because they are very similar, outboard and inboard (with a stern drive) care can be broken down into external, fuel systems, electrical, and the lower-end care—which includes the propeller.

Typically, the design and installation of the engine is engineered to occupy a very minimal amount of space. Outboards cram everything under one hood, and inboards put everything under the engine cowling. The roomiest compartments are probably on the midmount inboard engines. Usually the engine cover can be removed, revealing access to most of the engine components.

The standard inboard-outboard (or stern-drive) installation puts the engine at the back of the boat. The stern-drive unit needs to have access to the engine or transmission, through the transom of the boat. Therefore, the engine is mounted low in the engine compartment and close to the transom. That's often where the fuel tanks, bilge pump, batteries, and assorted other extras are installed. All of these things are then enclosed with a padded cover that doubles as a platform to stand on, or supports extra seating. In the end, it means a cramped and tight working area.

The best way to start working in the engine compartment is to get a couple of good work lights that can be positioned so that they totally illuminate the engine compartment. There are nooks and crannies all over the engine, and in the engine compartment. If you can't see, you can't find the problems. It is also important to have the proper tools.

Many engine compartments and engines look as good as the interior of the boat. *Bill Fedorko*

PROJECT 13 ★ *Engine Inspection*

When: Each time you take the boat out, or at least the beginning and end of season

Time: ½–2 hours

Tools: Shop lights and extension cords, or battery-operated flashlights; telescoping mechanics mirror (rectangular 2x3 inches is perfect) and small paintbrush to mark leaks; paintbrush or clean cloth for applying thinner or cleaner; wet/dry vacuum; wrench for loosening the alternator-adjustment bolts; pry bar or long screwdriver to use as a lever on alternator, or tension or adjustment roller

Supplies: Bright paint (or fingernail polish); acetone or paint thinner

Talent: ★★★★

Tab: $1–10

Tip: Cleaning before servicing is neater, but you might still need to clean after service to re move spills and stains. Twist the belts carefully and look closely at both sides for signs of wear or damage. Plan on replacing at any sign of deterioration (frayed fibers or cracks)

Gain: Lower risk of getting caught offshore with bad belts and possible engine damage

Before any cleaning or maintenance project, it's important to visually inspect the engine and the engine compartment, looking for any indications that additional service work might be required. To make a thorough inspection, you will need to have access to a telescoping mechanics mirror and a light or flashlight.

Starting at the top of the engine, remove the flame arrester or air cleaner assembly for better access to the fuel system. Shine the flashlight around the base of the carburetor, checking for signs of fuel leaks. Look for dark stains or damp areas.

Move around to view the cylinder heads and look for signs of oil or coolant leakage. This is where the

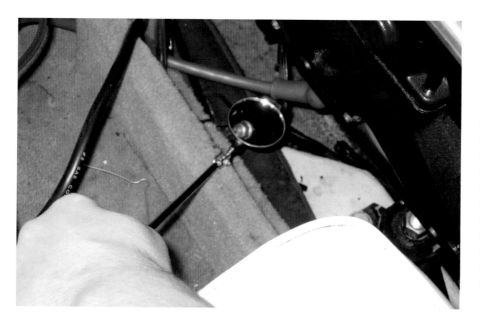

A 2x3-inch, rectangular telescoping mirror is the best, but you can use whatever you have. If necessary, you can use a larger mirror from the wall of your house and lay it down in the bilge area of the boat under the engine. The goal is to look around the lower areas for signs of leaks or damage. Shine a flashlight at the mirror and it should reflect on the engine.

If you see any leaks or signs of damage, it's best to mark them with a bright-colored paint or fingernail polish. After you wash the engine, you might not be able to see the leaks again. This way you will have the location marked, even if the leak is gone. The mark should remain after you repair the leak and be a reminder to check that area at the next inspection.

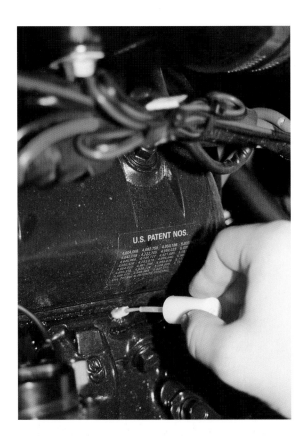

mirror comes in handy. Extend the handle of the mirror and place it low under the engine. Shine the flashlight on the mirror and look for moisture or stains that are visible on the bottom side of the cylinder heads, exhaust manifolds, and oil pan. Look for any signs of coolant leaks, oil, exhaust, or other stains. Without the mirror, you'll have to twist and crawl below the sides of the engine for a look. It probably can't be done effectively in most boats. Even if you can get a view, there will be a few areas that you just cannot see without the aid of the mirror. Note any problems such as stains, moisture, or cracks and where they were located.

Some owners like to mark the location of any leaks with a bright-colored paint or fingernail polish. If you take a brush or cloth moistened with paint

Check the belt's condition and tension by pushing on the belt at a halfway point between the two pulleys. If the belt moves more than ½ an inch, it should be tightened. Yes, you can buy a belt tension gauge, and your mechanic might have one. But if you follow the rule of thumb of about ½ an inch, you should be okay. Too much tension damages the shaft bearings in the alternator; too loose could let the belt slip or jump the pulley. Inspect the belt, top and bottom, looking for signs of damage, cracks, or loose fibers. Any damage could cause the belt to fail, usually when you are in the middle of the lake!

The belt's tension can usually be tightened by loosening the alternator and "prying" it away from the engine. Typically, the alternator has a small bolt attached to a slotted mount somewhere near the top of the alternator. At the bottom of the alternator is a pivot bolt. You might need to loosen the pivot bolt slightly before adjusting. Then loosen the adjustment bolt. With a large pry bar or screwdriver (big one, small ones will bend), pry the alternator out from the engine mounting bracket, tightening the belt. As you hold the alternator in its new position, tighten the top adjusting bolt. After that, tighten the pivot bolt at the bottom of the alternator. Check the belt tension again.

thinner or acetone, you can remove the oil or chemicals from the location that you need to mark. Make sure you are not applying paint thinner or acetone while the engine is hot! This is *dangerous*! These products must be used *only* on a cool engine block. Heat creates fire and explosions.

After the area has dried, mark the location of the leaks or stains with the paint. After marking, make sure you allow the paint to completely dry before you clean the engine. The reason for marking the past spots is so you will know where to look after the engine has been cleaned, the leaks repaired, and the test run completed. An inspection of the painted areas will be easier if they are visible, and you will be able to see if the leaks reappear.

Belt problems usually come too soon and belt maintenance comes too late. That is, the belts slip or break when you are the farthest from shore. The battery

goes dead; then the engine runs hot and the radio won't work. It is an experience that a boat owner should not have to endure. To prevent belt problems, regularly inspect the belts; make sure they are adjusted properly and that they are not cracking, wearing, or fraying. Any delaminating, loose fibers, or cracks in the belt should be noted and the belts must be replaced.

Today's belts are a lot better than the older models. Most of the older V-belts have been replaced by a new, flat design. While the quality is better, they still need to be inspected thoroughly.

Roll the belts in a couple of locations and look at the underside. If there are cracks or frayed areas, the belts should be replaced.

Pick a location halfway between two belt pulleys and press on the belt to see if it feels tight. You shouldn't be able to depress the belt more than about ½ to ¾ of an inch (check with your manufacturer's service manual).

51

While you are looking around under the engine, make sure the bilge pump is free from debris. Clean out any leaves or junk that might have collected around the intake. A blocked intake won't allow the water to be removed and could damage the bilge pump itself.

If the belt moves more than ¾ of an inch, it should be tightened. Take the appropriate wrench and loosen the bolt on the adjustment side of the alternator. Next, use the pry bar and lever the alternator to tighten the belt and retighten the adjustment bolt. Check the belt tension again. If you really want to get exact, you can purchase a belt tension gauge and test the belt. Typically, if you keep it under ¾ of an inch of movement, you shouldn't have any trouble.

After the overall engine and belt inspection is complete, check the bilge ventilation system. It depends on the date of manufacture, but most engine compartments are required to have a bilge ventilation system installed. The bilge ventilation system is designed to pump any fumes out of the engine compartment prior to starting. Any buildup of fuel

vapors in the bilge area could cause an explosion or fire. An inspection of the system not only includes putting your hand over the vent to make sure air is being pumped out, but inspecting the air intake to make sure it is clear of leaves, twigs, and debris that could be blocking the airflow. Make sure that you do not stack or store your life vests around the intake and block the flow of air.

The bilge pump should also be inspected at this time to make sure the pickup is not blocked with debris and any water that accumulates in the bilge area can be removed. You can clean this bilge area by hand or with a quality wet/dry vacuum. Commercial bilge cleaner is available to remove the grease, dirt, and grime from the area.

PROJECT 14 ★ *Wiring and Ignition Inspection*

When: Each time you take the boat out, or at least the beginning and end of season

Time: 1 hour

Tools: Flashlight; clean cloth

Supplies: New ignition-wire set

Talent: ★ ★ ★

Tab: $0–50 if new wires are needed

Tip: Soot or stains on the distributor cap or wires could indicate arcing

Gain: Efficiency and performance

After the belts are inspected, shine the flashlight on the distributor and the ignition wires. Ignition wires can get worn, cracked, or damaged, causing them to arc in areas along the engine. If the wires are in proximity to any metal, a closer inspection of that area should be made to look for worn spots or soot from arcing. Arcing can not only be a fire hazard, but it can reduce the voltage and current that makes it to the spark plugs. The current needs to flow all the way through the ignition wires, through the spark plug, and jump the spark plug gap in the cylinder. If the spark happens anywhere else, the spark plug will not be able to ignite the fuel mixture at its optimum level. Misfiring, poor fuel economy, and loss of power could be just a few of the symptoms.

As you trace the ignition wires, inspect the spark plug connectors and make sure that they fasten firmly to the spark plug top. Corrosion, worn caps, or loose connections are another performance stealer. If the spark plug cap cannot be connected firmly, it needs to be replaced.

If you locate a damaged area, the wire needs to be replaced. Spark plug wires should not be stiff or brittle. If they are stiff or inflexible, it is time to change them. Don't replace just one, but replace the complete set of ignition wires. Most boat dealers or automotive

This alternator is still working, but it shows signs of rust and corrosion.

Remove the spark plug wires one at a time and inspect the cap, looking for signs of arcing, soot, or oil.

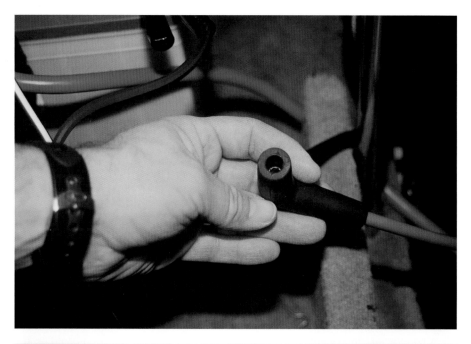

Anywhere the wires are clumped together, sharply bent, or wire-tied is a potential spot for damage. Wires with tight bends can become stiff and brittle, causing the insulation to crack or break the wire. Any wire ties or groups of wires can rub together or against surrounding metal, causing worn areas, damage, and potential shorts in the electrical circuits.

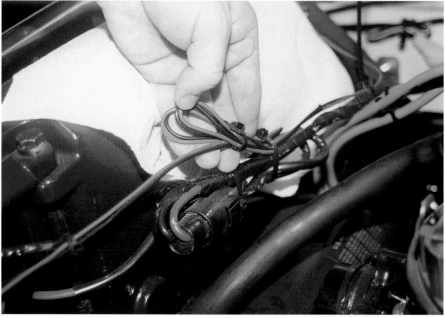

supply companies can provide you with a set of ignition wires.

If you don't find any arcing or damaged areas, you can wipe the ignition wires down with a cloth to remove any moisture, oil, or dirt. Too much oil or grease on the wires can cause deterioration of the wire insulation and premature failure.

If your engine is still running a distributor ignition system (many are), you can remove the distributor cap, inspect it for signs of arcing in areas other than the contacts, and then wipe the inside with a dry cloth. If there are lines of soot or arc evidence, the distributor cap needs to be replaced.

If you are changing the ignition wires and the distributor cap, remember to mark the wires and where they attach to the distributor cap (if the cap is not marked) so that you can get the plug wires in the correct firing order. Nothing will ruin a trip to the water more than an engine that coughs, sputters, and backfires— except maybe the ribbing and heckling your friends and family will bestow upon you when you explain that you connected the spark plug wires wrong.

PROJECT 15 ★ *Spark Plugs*

When: Beginning and end of season

Time: 2–3 hours

Tools: ⅜-inch ratchet; assorted-length ⅜ extensions; ⅜-inch universal joint; spark plug socket (usually ⅝ or ¹³⁄₁₆); spark plug gap tool; spark plug cleaner (or small wire bristle brush); cordless Dremel tool and wire brush bits

Supplies: New replacement spark plugs; thread compound

Talent: ★ ★ ★ ★

Tab: $25–40

Tip: New spark plugs still need to have the gap checked prior to installation

Gain: Better fuel economy and performance

Spark plugs are an internal combustion engine's fuel igniter in the cylinder. If the spark plugs are dirty, improperly adjusted, or faulty, the engine may not operate at its peak performance and efficiency. Today's spark plugs can last for years.

Automotive manufacturers are claiming hundreds of thousands of miles on the same spark plugs. While that may be possible in an automobile, it is not as probable in boat. Yes, spark plugs can and do last a long time in a boat, as owners who ignore them can

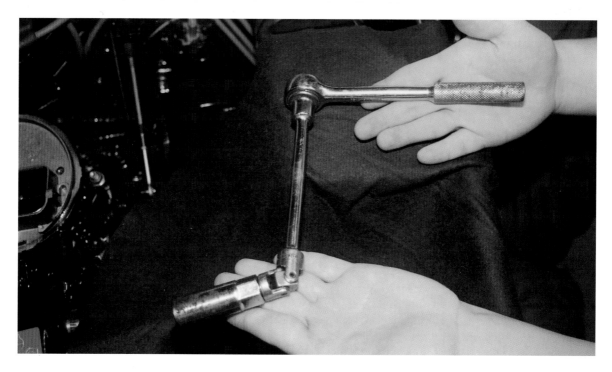

A ⅜-inch ratchet, extension, universal, and spark plug socket will reach most inboard locations. Make sure you use the correct spark plug socket. Some have a rubber grommet in the socket to help prevent the spark plug from breaking.

When removing the spark plug, try to keep the extensions as straight as possible. Any time you have the ratchet at an angle from the socket, you risk slipping on the plug and breaking the ceramic portion of the plug. (Ask my son.)

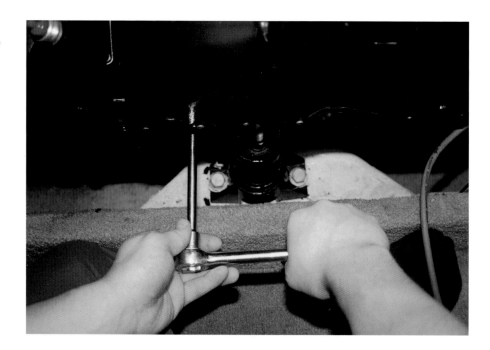

If you are not replacing the plugs, you can clean them with a spark plug cleaner, a Dremel tool with a wire brush bit, or with a hand brush as shown here.

attest, but the lifestyle of a boat versus a car dictates that a boat's plugs have a shorter lifespan. Boats run infrequently, and they typically operate at higher power settings. Because of the use and abuse marine spark plugs can endure, it is recommended that they be inspected (and possibly changed) occasionally.

If you are planning to change or adjust your spark plugs, it's well worth the cost to buy a spark plug socket, a universal joint, ratchet, and a couple of different-length extensions. The spark plug socket is a deep socket, deep enough to go over the top of the spark plug and reach the metal base of the plug. There is a rubber grommet inserted into the socket to lower the risk of breaking the porcelain top of the spark plug. The rubber grommet will center the spark plug's porcelain top, and keep it from contacting the socket sidewalls. Be careful when removing spark plugs; one small slip can snap the porcelain top.

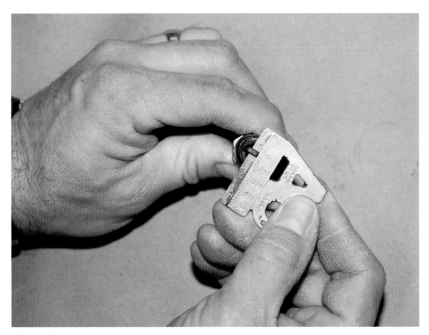

Spark plugs need to have the gap (distance between the center electrode and the outside electrode) set before installation. Used plugs will be worn and corroded, so the gap may be larger than the manufacturer's recommendation. This could cause misfiring and inefficient operation. New plugs are preset from the factory, but the gap may need to be changed for your specific use. The engine service manual should have the correct measurements for your engine. The gap can be set with "feeler" gauges, a wire gap tool, or the slide gap tool as shown.

Before installing a spark plug, the threads should be coated with an anti-seize compound. This will keep the spark plugs from getting corroded and "seizing" the threads in the spark plug holes.

To remove, you'll need the proper ratchet size. Your owner's manual should provide you with the correct specifications. First, remove the spark plug wire's end cap, and slip the spark plug socket over the spark plug. Make sure it fits firmly over the top of the spark plug, and all the way over the metal spark plug's base.

After fitting the socket on the spark plug, attach the universal joint to the socket and an appropriate extension to the universal joint. Attach the ratchet to the extension. By grasping the universal joint area with one hand, and the ratchet with your other hand, give the ratchet a twist. This should loosen the spark plug. Remember, to loosen spark plugs, turn them counterclockwise. One way to remember is the old line "lefty loosey, righty tighty."

The initial pressure will be the highest. The spark plugs have been tightened into the cylinder head, and the heat has expanded and contracted the material. If the previous plug wasn't treated with thread compound, the threads could be corroded. Don't use an unusual amount of force to remove the spark plug. If the spark plug is stuck, you do not want to break it and damage the engine. Take the boat to a mechanic and have him or her complete the job.

After you have removed the spark plug, look at it under the light to determine its condition. The spark plugs can tell you how the engine is running. The different colors of the soot and the shape of the electrodes are an indication if the engine is getting the proper fuel and air mixture, if the engine is leaking oil, or even if there is a moisture problem.

Most service manuals will have a sample of what a correct burning plug should look like. Typically, the spark plug should be a light tan or gray color. If it is black and sooty looking, it could be a sign of a too rich (too much) fuel mixture or too cold of a plug. A very light color, almost white, may indicate that the spark plug is too hot for the use or the fuel mixture is too lean (too little fuel). A shiny black or oily coating may indicate that there is a seal problem that allows too much oil into the cylinders. If you are unsure, you may want to take the spark plugs to the mechanic for an opinion.

Cleaning the old spark plug can be done with a spark plug cleaner. This is a small box that is like a minisandblaster. Put the plug in the opening, turn it on, and the unit blasts the dirt, carbon, and crud from the electrode end of the spark plug. If you do not have a spark plug cleaner, you can use a wire brush to clean the carbon and soot from the plug. You can also use a small piece of emery cloth or sandpaper to clean the end of the center electrode and side electrode. Then use a very small file to file the ends of the electrodes. Of course, you can use the cordless Dremel with a wire brush bit to clean the plugs. If you haven't noticed, the Dremel is a great tool to have in your toolbox. After it is cleaned, you set the gap and reinstall.

An easier way to clean plugs is to replace them. Just buy new plugs! New plugs should have the electrode gap measured to make sure they are correct for your engine prior to installation. The plug threads should have thread compound applied, and then the plug should be started in the spark plug hole. This can be done by hand with the plug alone, or by inserting the plug into the socket and starting the installation. Always start the plug and tighten it by hand as far as possible before using the ratchet. The reason for this is to make sure the plug threads are started correctly. If you install the plug with the ratchet and you do not get the threads started straight, you could damage the cylinder head threads. Cross-threading will require major engine work to correct the problem. Start by hand and don't take that chance.

After the plug is installed finger-tight, attach the extension, universal, and ratchet-tighten it more. Some people (and possibly your service manual) will recommend using a torque wrench to tighten the plug. Many of the mechanics I know tighten the plug using the leverage of the ratchet handle, until it requires exerting "pressure," then they give it ¼ to ½ a turn more. This might take a little practice. The plug needs to be tight, but not too tight.

After the spark plug is installed, reattach the plug wire. Make sure the plug wire cap is firmly in place.

PROJECT 16 ★ *Engine Service*

When: Beginning and end of season

Time: ½–1 hour

Tools: Small grease gun

Supplies: Waterproof marine grease; WD-40 spray lubricant

Talent: ★★

Tab: $25

Tip: Make sure you use the manufacturer's service manual to locate all of the grease zerks

Gain: Longer bushing and bearing life, smoother operation

As you went through the initial inspection of the engine compartment and the engine, you should have seen the grease fittings, along with the transmission and the control cable, and linkage attachment points. You might also have seen the steering components (hydraulic pump, hoses and cylinders or cables and connectors). These areas will all need to be lubricated or greased.

Inspect the transmission and shifter linkage. Make sure the linkages are free to move, and adjusted for the correct movement as recommended by the manufacturer's service manual. Lubricate the connections

The hydraulic lower-end tilt needs to be inspected for loose wires or hoses. Look for leaks or any damage.

After removing the red cap, fill the hydraulic oil with the manufacturer's recommended brand and weight. After the reservoir is filled, replace the cap.

If everything seems to be going wrong with your engine, it just might be time to remove it from the boat. This engine was going through a number of problems. The electrical system was not functioning correctly, the bellows were damaged by water leaking into the gimble and universal area, and the universal joint in the lower end was rusted almost solid. The engine itself needed to be overhauled. The advantage to this extreme step is the access to the bilge area and transom.

and linkages. If the fittings have grease fittings, use the grease gun. If not, use WD-40. WD-40 is a water-disbursement lubricant; it helps remove moisture and lubricates at the same time.

You will want to use a grease gun with marine waterproof grease (as recommended by the manufacturer) to service the gimble bearing and spline joint.

Another service that needs to be done, but should probably be left to the mechanic, is aligning the driveshaft. When doing this, the stern drive is removed and a spare driveshaft is inserted into the transmission or engine. The alignment of the transmission and the shaft is adjusted for smooth operation and reduced wear on the transmission or engine, shaft, and stern drive.

Spray all the linkages with a good silicone lubricant or WD-40. WD-40 can help remove moisture from the area and lubricate the surfaces at the same time.

PROJECT 17 ★ *Oil Change*

When: Every 25 hours or each season

Time: 2 hours

Tools: Oil-filter wrench; oil-change kit (pump and container for disposal); can opener; magnet

Supplies: Oil, required amount per manufacturer's service manual

Talent: ★★★

Tab: $25

Tip: Place an oil-absorption mat in the bilge area to collect drips and leaks

Gain: Improved engine life and better engine cooling

Everyone should know about oil and oil changes. The oil in the engine is used to lubricate all the moving metal engine parts, but it does more than just lubricate. It carries particles of dirt contaminants and heat away from the moving parts. As the oil moves throughout the engine and does all this work, it is sent through a filter that collects as much of the sediment and gunk as possible.

Oil does not last forever. After a while the chemical makeup of the oil starts to break down. It collects soot, fills up with acids, and the oil just doesn't work as well. One major problem is the oil can't carry the same amount of heat as it did before. In turn, that can allow the engine to run at higher temperatures and break the oil down further. It's time for an oil change. Sure, there are a few oil manufacturers that claim their oils can last hundreds of thousands of miles without breaking down. There are oil additives that are supposed to extend the life of the oil and the time between oil changes, but let's face the facts. If you have to put additives in the oil to make it last longer, it must be missing something. The old oil needs to be removed, the filter needs changing, and the new oil gets installed.

Oil changes are a simple and inexpensive maintenance item that can save lots of money in the long run. Regularly changing the oil keeps the inside of the engine clean, lubricated, and running smoothly. It's also a good time to check for any metal particles in the oil that might indicate a wearing or breakdown in the engine.

Most boat service manuals recommend changing oil every 25 to 50 hours of operation or every six months, depending on how much the boat is used. Only four-cycle outboards have a need for oil in the crankcase. Two-cycle engines use oil injectors or oil mixed in the fuel to provide the lubrication.

When you change the oil, find a licensed oil-disposal service to take your used oil. Many auto supply stores have a drop-off location for used oil. It isn't free, but you are disposing of the oil in a safe and legal manner. Improper disposal is illegal in most states and is very bad for the environment.

Most engines have a drain plug on the bottom of the oil pan. However, if you simply remove the drain plug, the oil will just run into the bilge area of the boat, causing a cosmetic mess and an environmental hazard.

There are quick drain adapters that can be installed in place of the drain plug. These quick drains connect to a drain hose that runs out the back of the boat through the transom drain. The valve can be open and closed to control the flow of the oil. While definitely better than just draining the oil into the bottom of the boat, this method has its disadvantages. For one, you have to attach the drain hose and get it through the transom drain, you still need a container for the used oil, and it still drips in the bottom of the boat while you are trying to get the hose disconnected. Plus, it is difficult to get under the engine to connect everything and turn on the valve. If you have one of the newer engines, they often come from the factory with a quick-drain kit already installed.

To do a good oil change, you should run the engine and warm the oil, which means as you are trying to reach under the exhaust manifold and down below the hot crankcase to the oil drain, you'll have the risk

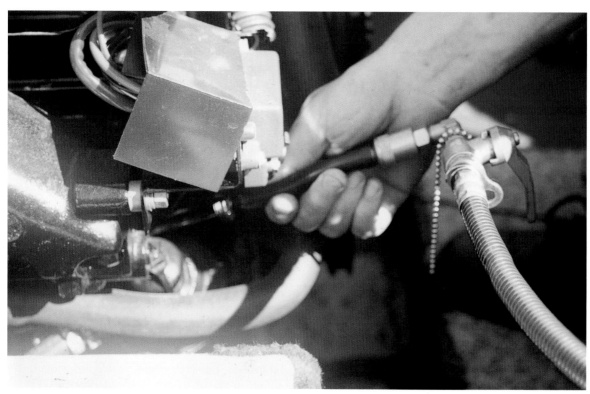

Depending on the manufacturer's design, the oil pump can be connected to a specifically designed fitting on the crankcase or . . . attached to a fitting on the dip-stick tube.

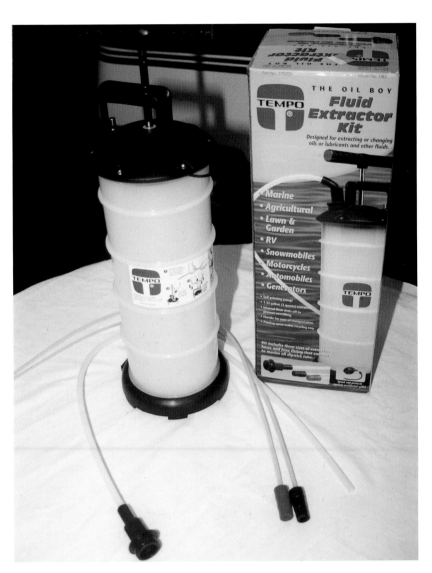

The Tempo Oil Boy Fluid Extractor Kit does the same as the powered units, but costs less and uses the "arm strong" method of removal. The kit comes with the storage tank, a pump, and assorted fittings for different applications. If you have the fittings built into the crankcase or need the filler tube adapters, the Oil Boy comes ready to go.

of being burned or at least singed. There are also reported failures of the quick drains that have leaked or opened and drained the engine oil at inopportune times, ruining the engine. Don't take this as a reason not to use a quick-drain kit. Aircraft have been installing quick drains for years with very few problems.

However, there is another way.

Numerous companies manufacture oil-change kits that siphon or pump the oil out of the engine through the dip-stick tube. There are manual or electric pumps. The economical manual pumps cost from $20 to $60. Tempo Products makes a very economical and well-built oil pump. The Oil Boy Fluid Extractor Kit is made from heavy plastic and comes with all the fittings you should need for the majority of boats. The kit includes the garden-hose-sized fittings for the Volvo Penta 4.3 that we drained. The kit

also included the small tube to slide in the dip-stick drain on the older Mercruiser. Assorted boats, assorted fittings—the Oil Boy is capable of handling all of them.

If you plan on changing the oil while the boat is in the water, this is probably going to be the only way to get it done. The pump system extracts the oil from the engine and stores it in the tank of the pump. The pumps are designed with a handle and are transportable, so you can haul the oil to a disposal location. You do not want to spill the oil into the water and create the surface slick (and environmental hazard) that everyone at the lake remembers you by.

To drain the oil, it needs to be warmed. Logically, it would be best to hook up the flushing system and run the engine for a few minutes, or change the oil after you returned to the dock. Do not drain the oil

Once the applicable drain fittings are attached or inserted, you pump up and down on the handle to remove the oil. Remember, the oil needs to be warm, but not hot. The Tempo Oil Boy Fluid Extractor Kit will withstand some heat, but not extreme temperatures.

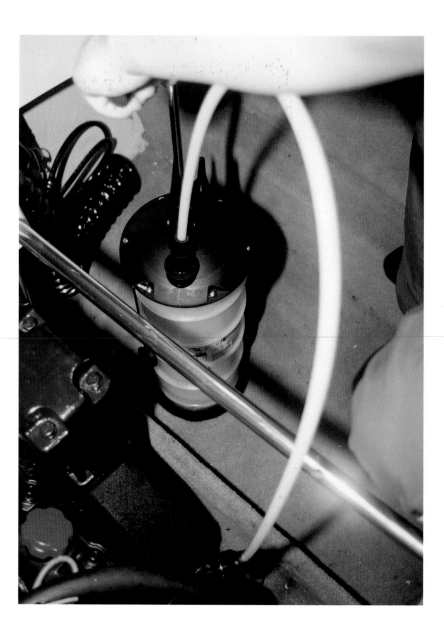

when it is hot, just warm. Warming the oil thins the viscosity and allows the oil to drain from the engine components back into the oil pan. Additionally, since these pumps draw the oil through the dip-stick tube, you can imagine that the tube is very small. The oil needs to be thinned for the pump to draw it through the tube. Many of the pump kits are made from plastic, and if the oil is too hot, it will melt the container and pump.

After the oil is warmed, remove the oil filler cap, usually located on top of one of the valve covers. Remove the dipstick, insert the tube per the manufacturer's instructions, and start pumping.

On four-cycle outboards, use the manufacturer's service guidelines to locate the lower drain plug.

Make sure you have a way to catch the used oil in a reclamation container. You can use the Oil Boy Fluid Extractor Kit and remove the oil through the dipstick tube, as on an inboard. (Check out the location of the dipstick in the cutaway picture.) Or, you can remove the drain plug and open the oil filler cap. Let the old oil drain from the engine per the manufacturer's recommended procedures.

After the old oil is removed, but before the new oil is installed, you will need to replace the oil filter. Most filters are of the screw-on variety. That means they look kind of like a metal can, with a threaded fitting on one end. They are filled with a paper material that allows the oil to pass through the paper, but stops and collects any small particles in the folds of the

Inboard engines are typically a variation of an automotive engine. Adding oil is just a process of removing the filler cap and putting in quart after quart of oil. Each engine can hold different amounts, typically about six quarts, so make sure you know what your engine holds. Check your service manual for the correct amount, type, and weight of oil to use.

paper. The filters are usually just a little too tight to get off by hand; that's where the filter wrench comes in handy. A few filters have a nut shape built onto the top of the filter. If the filter has that, all you need is a ratchet and socket or an open-end wrench of the same size.

If the filter is smooth on the top, use the band-style wrench to remove it. The band style has a handle and a rubber, metal, or chain band that is attached to the end of the handle. There is a small section of the handle that moves and loosens the band so that it will fit over the filter. After the belt is slipped over the filter, move the lever in the direction to loosen the filter (typically counterclockwise, or to the left). The band tightens around the filters (the metal housing) and grips the filter, allowing it to unscrew.

The filter will still have a little oil in it. Filters will not usually drain completely out when you drain the oil because they hang sideways (or upside down below the engine case), so be careful to remove it without tipping it over and spilling used oil all over the inside of the boat.

Drain the filter through a funnel into the waste oil container. While the filter is draining, reverse the procedure to install the new filter. Filters should be inspected to make sure they are not damaged before installation. There is an O-ring or flat gasket that seals the outside edge of the filter against the engine's case. Make sure you put a light film of high-temperature grease on this O-ring so it doesn't dry out, stick, and become damaged while installing. If you do not have any grease you can use a coating of oil, but it doesn't last as long as the grease does.

Install the filter finger-tight. Screw the filter in place as tight as possible by hand, then reverse the direction of the filter wrench and give it about a ½ to ¾ turn more.

After the filter is installed, you can add the new oil. If you bought quart containers of oil, open one at a time and start pouring them into the oil fill opening (usually the spot on the valve cover). Fill the engine (with the manufacturer's recommended

From this cutaway engine picture, you can see the dip stick for checking the oil in a four-cycle outboard motor.

amount of oil), insert the dipstick firmly in place, then remove and read the oil level.

If you are interested in what the inside of the filter looks like, use an old can opener to cut the end of the filter off (cut the end that has the screw-in threads). After removing the end, you will want to slide the paper filter out slowly so that you can see what type of particles are trapped in the paper filter. Unroll the filter on a flat surface. You can always put newspaper under it to help collect the oil. Pass a magnet over the paper and see if it picks up any pieces of metal. An experienced mechanic would be able to tell you where the metal was from.

Certain types of material and shapes would indicate wear on a certain part of the engine. For example, larger shards of ferrous metal (that the magnet picks up) are probably from the crank or the camshaft. Smaller fragments, more like pepper of nonferrous metal, would probably indicate wear on the bushings.

If you find any larger pieces of metal or foreign material in the filter or in your oil, take it to a mechanic. Any signs of wear or deterioration need to be checked out by a professional. An engine inspection now could save you from getting stuck on the lake *and* spare you overhaul costs.

PROJECT 18 ★ *Battery Service*

When: Every 50 hours or each season

Time: ½ hour

Tools: Battery-post cleaning brush; cordless Dremel tool and wire brush; stiff-bristle brush; battery charger

Supplies: Baking soda; distilled water; protective battery terminal spray; water

Talent: ★ ★

Tab: $20

Tip: Use a lot of freshwater when cleaning to flush the battery and dilute the corrosion residue

Gain: Reduces the damage to battery case and surrounding surfaces

The battery is needed to start the engine, operate the lights, and play the stereo, not to mention all the other accessories that use battery electricity to operate. The battery is continually charged by the engine's charging (alternator) system. A battery cannot do its job unless it is clean, filled with acid and water, and has corrosion-free connections.

Terminal cleaning brushes are available at most auto or discount stores like Wal-Mart. The brush has stiff wire fibers in the opening that clean the terminal when the brush is pushed over the post and turned back and forth. The other end is a small wire brush that can be inserted into the terminal clamp and used to clean corrosion on the inside of the terminal clamp. The Dremel tool with the wire brush is also an excellent way to clean the post and clamps.

Baking soda sprinkled on top of the battery and mixed with water helps to clean the corrosion and dirt from the battery case. Use enough baking soda and water to create a paste.

With an old paintbrush or a disposable stiff-bristle brush, work the baking soda mixture all over the case.

Rinse the battery housing with lots of freshwater to remove the baking soda and dirt.

If your battery is a refillable type, open the caps and check the level of water in the cells. Fill the cells to the full line with distilled water. An old squeeze bottle makes a handy dispenser.

After each trip, the battery should be stored fully charged. A fully charged battery will not freeze in cold weather. A battery with a low charge will allow the plates inside the battery to get a buildup on them and deteriorate.

If your boat is equipped with lots of electrical items such as GPS, VHF radios, stereos systems, live well or bait aerators, and fish finders, you need to use marine "deep-cycle" batteries. Regular batteries are designed to generate current in a short burst, as when you are starting the engine. A deep-cycle battery is designed to provide smaller amounts of power for a longer period of time.

It's also recommended that you have a dual battery system. This is especially helpful if you travel a great distance from your home base. Two batteries will offer twice as much power. Additionally, you can have a system setup that allows you to manually or automatically select which battery you use and charge.

The first thing to do is make a good visual inspection of the battery and its connections. Look for any signs of arcing (dark sooty areas) from the battery posts to any close wires or cables. Look for worn areas on the battery exterior (case), signs of leakage, or cracks. If there are any visible signs of wear, replace the battery immediately. The acid in the battery is extremely corrosive and dangerous.

Check the cables for damage, worn areas, or frayed wires. Check the connections to make sure the ends are firmly attached to the cables.

Clean the battery case and terminals with a mixture of baking soda and water. Sprinkle the baking soda across the top of the battery and the terminals. Sprinkle water on the battery and clean with a small, stiff-bristled brush. Scrub the battery and terminals firmly and rinse the mixture with lots of clean water.

After the battery is clean, coat the terminals with an insulating film of grease or petroleum jelly. You can also install "anti-corrosive washers" (felt washers coated with a corrosion-prevention chemical), or spray the terminals and cable ends with a protective battery spray.

Make sure that you clean the corrosion from the cable ends. If you have the type of ends that fit over the post, use the post-clamp cable cleaning brush *or* the cordless Dremel tool with a wire brush to clean the inside of the clamp. You can also use this wire brush on the terminals of the battery, and on any other type of cable ends, to remove corrosion and provide a better contact surface.

If the battery is the type that can have the caps removed, check its water level. If low, refill with distilled water. If the battery is the sealed type, you cannot check the fluid level.

Many manufacturers recommend that you put a charger on your batteries after you return from a trip. Not a small trickle charger, but a good 10–15-amp charger. Make sure the batteries are back up to 100 percent.

The charging system on most engines should charge the batteries sufficiently, if they are being used on a regular basis. If you park the boat for several days between uses, the batteries may not get fully charged. Batteries that are not fully charged can get buildup on the internal parts that will reduce their capacity and their power output.

Anytime you are planning on leaving your boat alone for an extended period of time (over the winter or just in storage), it's a good idea to remove the battery and store it in a safe, dry place. Check battery fluid levels and make sure it is fully charged. If you are not removing it, at least unhook the negative or ground cable to disconnect the circuit while it is parked. Many of the electronic items in the boat drain the battery over time.

PROJECT 19 ★ *Fuel Systems*

When: Every 25 hours or each season

Time: 2–3 hours

Tools: Screwdriver; combination wrench to remove flame arrester; combination wrench for removing fuel filter; fuel-proof drip pan; fire extinguisher; screwdriver or nut driver for removal of clamps

Supplies: Replacement fuel separator/filter; ValvTect Marine Engine Injector Cleaner

Talent: ★★★

Tab: $45

Tip: Always disconnect the battery before working on the fuel system to eliminate un wanted sparks

Gain: Better economy and performance

Depending on your outboard, the fuel filter may be in the fuel line or part of the fuel system. There may also be a water separator/filter mounted remotely, as in the inboard section.

If there is a fuel filter mounted in the fuel line start by disconnecting the fuel line. You do not want fuel siphoning out of the tank while you have the fuel line open.

The clear type of fuel filters can be removed by hand, replaced, or cleaned. One advantage is that you should be able to see sediment or buildup in the clear bowl.

71

The arrester is designed to help reduce the temperature of fuel vapors exiting the intake because of something like a backfire, reducing or preventing the risk of fire in the engine compartment. It also acts like an air filter and will get dirty. You can replace it or clean it. If the arrester is extremely dirty, you may want to replace it. If not, you can use a cleaning solvent to remove the grease and dirt. Spray the arrester from the inside out, blowing the dirt and solvent from the metal "filter." Make sure that you have removed any solvent and moisture from the arrester before reinstalling on the engine.

If the filter is attached with worm-gear clamps, as in many of the older outboards, place the drip pan under the filter and loosen the clamps with the appropriate screwdriver or nut driver. These older style filters are throwaway. That is, you remove them from the system and toss them in the garbage. A new filter is inserted in the line, and the clamps tighten to seal the hose and prevent leaks. Make sure the filter is inserted with the flow of the fuel going the correct direction. Usually there is an indication as to the direction (an arrow) or a label indicating the inlet of the filter.

If you have a replaceable filter, use the appropriate size of wrench to disassemble the filter housing so you can remove the filter from the housing. Replace the filter and reassemble the housing.

After the filter is reinstalled in the fuel system, connect the fuel line, pressurize the system, and check for leaks.

When you look at the inboard engine, you usually see a large, circular item (sometimes rectangular) that looks like an air filter. That's the flame arrester. Yes, it does filter air that comes into the carburetor, but its main design is to stop flames from getting out of the carburetor.

Any internal combustion engine needs three components to run: fuel, oxygen, and ignition. The ignition comes from the coil and spark plugs, the oxygen comes from the atmosphere (through the air filter/flame arrester), and the fuel comes from the fuel tank.

The vaporized gasoline entering the intake sometimes is vented back through the carburetor and into the engine compartment. These vapors will be vented from the engine compartment into the atmosphere with the use of the bilge ventilation system. Until they are vented they really pose no threat, *unless*

Some engines use an inline fuel filter. Plastic fuel filters should never be used unless they are installed by the factory. If you are using a metal filter, it is difficult to see when the filter is clogged or dirty. You should replace the filter at regular intervals to prevent getting stuck on the lake. Again, make sure the battery is disconnected and the engine is cold before changing the filter. When you remove the worn gear clamps, fuel is likely to drip from the lines and a hot engine could cause a fire. Have the new filter ready to install before you loosen the hose clamps. Loosen one end clamp on the old filter, remove that end of the old filter from the fuel line, and immediately install the new filter in the line. Loosen the other hose clamp on the old filter, remove the old filter, and immediately attach the hose directly to the new filter. This should reduce the amount of fuel that will drain from the lines during the process. It also helps to put a small drip pan under the filter to collect any lost fuel for disposal.

there is a source of ignition.

Many fires are caused because the fuel vapors were ignited when the inboard engine backfired. This risk prompted the U.S. government to actually require that any inboard gasoline engine be equipped with an approved "flame arrester."

If the engine ignites the fuel in the intake systems (e.g., you suddenly reduce the throttle, or during starting the engine backfires), the vapors in the intake explode or ignite. The expanding and burning fuel exits the intake through the path of least resistance, which is usually going "out" the intake and carburetor. If an automotive-style paper air filter is installed on the engine, the resulting flames will shoot right through the paper and ignite any fuel

vapors that are lingering in the engine compartment. That's where the flame arrester comes in. The flame arrester is made of small pieces of metals, bonded or pressed very tightly together. Air will still pass through the porous material, but as it does, it slows down and cools in temperature. The lower temperature helps to contain the fire or even extinguish it. Therefore, any fuel vapors that are outside the engine will not have a source of ignition.

Seem complicated? Don't worry about it. All you need to know is that your inboard engine has an approved and undamaged flame arrester installed. Do not replace it with an automotive-style air filter. Inspect the flame arrester and look for any damage that has created a hole that the flame can

73

sneak through. Make sure yours is in good condition. Replace it if there are any doubts.

Okay, moving on to the fuel system. The fuel is pumped from the fuel tank to the carburetor, or injector system, and then it has to go though the intake system and/or into the cylinders for ignition at just the correct time.

Of course, if anything gets into the fuel, the fuel doesn't ignite or the fuel doesn't flow. For that reason, there needs to be a system in place to control the contaminants in the fuel. Since a boat spends most of its time on the water, water can be a number one contaminant. There are fuel filters and fuel water separators. Most of today's boats need (or have) a combination water separator and fuel filter. The separator filter should be drained and cleaned regularly.

Depending on the type of system installed on the boat, it may be as simple as spinning off the filter. A typical separator does just what the name says; it separates the heavier water molecules and traps them in a "container." The water can be drained from the separator via a valve on the bottom. The fuel also passes through a filter to remove any contaminants that might be in the system. Dirt, bugs, and fibers can all block the fuel flow in the carburetor or the injection system. These items are also collected in the filter and can be removed by cleaning or changing the filter.

If the fuel tank caps "pool" water after a rain or a run on rough water, make sure the gaskets sealing the cap are in good shape. If not, the water will drain into the fuel tank and ultimately get into the fuel lines.

Before you remove the water separator/fuel filter, always make sure the engine is cool and there is a fire extinguisher nearby. Anytime you work with a fuel system part there is the risk of fuel leaking, or vapors escaping, and the potential for fire. A spark from static electricity, an electrical component, or the light that shines on the area can ignite any small leaks. Like a good scout, always be prepared!

If your water separator has a valve that can be used to drain it, just place a container under the valve and drain away. If it has to be removed, make sure that you shut the fuel off. There should be a fuel shut-off valve in the system. If not, it's time to take the boat to a mechanic and let him make the fuel filter change, or add a fuel shutoff.

Replace the water separator/fuel filter with a new filter, turn on the fuel, and look for leaks.

If your system has a fuel filter in the fuel line, it's a little more complicated and a little messy. The filter in the line will have to be removed by removing the clamps or fittings on each end of the filter.

The air filter needs to be removed and inspected. If it shows any signs of dirt or grime, it must be replaced. Make sure you replace it with a spark-resistant filter. This will help prevent a fire if the engine ever decides to cough and shoot fuel back out of the intake and into the filter.

If your engine has an injection system and is computer controlled, you should take it to the service center for repairs. Many of the newer boats need to have specialized testing equipment and tools. Don't take the chance of screwing up a perfectly good engine, just to save a few bucks. If you want to do a little preventive maintenance, pour a bottle of ValvTect Marine Engine Injector Cleaner (or a similar additive) into the fuel tank and run it through the system. The additive will help clean the injectors and all the components it runs through.

PROJECT 20 ★ *Engine Compartment Cleaning*

When: At minimum, the beginning and end of each season

Time: 1–2 hours

Tools: Stiff-bristle, long-handled cleaning brush; water hose; spray nozzle

Supplies: Spray degreaser and water

Talent: ★ ★

Tab: $15–25

Tip: Do not saturate or use high pressure on the electrical components (distributor, coil and wires, or computer). If possible, cover the engine computer or distributor with a plastic bag before spraying the engine

Gain: Better-looking engine, easier to check for leaks

All you have to do is warm the engine (it should still be warm from the oil change) and spray the engine degreaser all over the engine block and valve covers. Give the engine a good coat of the degreaser. Remember, it's best to stay away from the coil, distributor, and other electrical components.

After a coat of the degreaser, scrub the greasy and dirty areas with the stiff-bristle brush. After you have loosened the grime and crud, spray the engine with the water and rinse away the messy mixture. Do not spray directly on the ignition components, or the engine might not start. Make sure the boat is at an angle (bow high) to allow the water and degreaser solution to drain out the transom drain and into a bucket. If you are in a slip, this stuff shouldn't be pumped into the water. The best way is to use a wet/dry vacuum or leave the job until the boat can be dry-docked.

Oil and grease can deteriorate wires, belts, and hoses. Grease can stiffen linkages, causing bent cables or stuck throttles. Spraying degreaser can keep the excess dirt and grime to a minimum. Any degreaser available from a local discount or auto parts store will work. Spray the engine liberally, being careful not to coat the distributor and electrical components directly. Follow the instructions on the degreaser for the best results. Some products work best if the engine has been warmed slightly to help soften the grease and oil with heat before the degreaser is applied. Once the degreaser is used, spray the engine with freshwater from a hose and spray nozzle. High-pressure power washing might be better to remove the grease, but it can often damage accessories or force water into areas that you really do not want to get wet. Low pressure from a garden hose works the best.

This engine compartment is immaculate. To get these results will take considerable time, but it will also be well worth it.

PROJECT 21 ★ *Cooling System Flush*

When: Each time you take the boat out

Time: 1–2 hours

Tools: Earmuff-style engine flush kit; water hose

Supplies: Access to water

Talent: ★ ★ ★

Tab: $25

Tip: Flushing the system after every use, even freshwater use, removes sediment and dirt

Gain: Lowers risk of internal corrosion and water-pump damage

It doesn't matter whether you have a stern drive or an outboard, or whether you are using your boat in saltwater or freshwater—it is always a good idea to flush the system with freshwater. This is a very simple procedure when you have the correct equipment.

Purchase a quality earmuff-style flushing adapter (which costs from $15 to $30) that fits on the lower unit water pickup (or flushing port, when available). They are available from most local marine dealers, online marine supply stores, and have even been spotted at discount stores like Wal-Mart in the sporting goods department. A few stern drives and outboards have a flushing adapter built into the engine, so the earmuff style is not necessary.

Once the flushing adapter is installed, attach a garden hose, turn on the water, and start the engine.

The earmuff adapter should be installed from the front of the lower unit. This keeps the earmuff adapter out of the way of the propeller, should it idle along. A few of the mechanics I talked to and a couple of the earmuff instructions state to remove the propeller before starting the engine.

Do not turn the hose on at high pressure or you could damage the water-pump impeller. Set the water pressure at half-pressure and run your engine at idle speed (in neutral). Try to run the engine for at least 5 minutes to flush out any salt and sediment. Your outboard motor owner's manual should give you information about this specific procedure for your engine.

Remember, flushing the cooling system is a good thing to do after every operation, especially after the engine is operated in saltwater.

Almost every boat supply or discount store has an earmuff flush kit available. Most owners should invest in one since it is recommended by most manufacturers to flush the engines after every use. Flushing prevents the buildup of sediment, corrosion, or saltwater. The earmuff unit is forced over the lower unit until it covers the water intake openings.

Once the flushing adapter is located over the intake openings, attach a hose and turn the water on to a medium level. Do not use high pressure or you could damage the water pump. Start the engine and let it run at idle speed for at least 5 minutes. Different manufacturers have different opinions about leaving the propeller on or off. Many opt for removal. Check for the manufacturer's recommendation.

It doesn't matter if you have one stern drive, two stern drives, or an outboard motor, the process is the same. Connect the flush adapter, connect the hoses, turn on the water, and idle the engines. *Bill Fedorko*

SECTION 4

STERN-DRIVE AND OUTBOARD

Projects 22 through 25

The inboard-outboard was a great invention. It allowed boat manufacturers to place higher-performance, higher-horsepower automotive-style engines in the boat. The reliability of the automobile engine and its technological advances could be incorporated into the boat design, and the engine could still be mounted toward the rear of the boat, providing more usable cockpit space. Auto-style engines have been used with inboard boats for years, but most required a mounting location that was toward the middle of the boat, and a driveshaft that was susceptible to bending and vibration. The stern-drive

The bellows in this lower unit developed a leak and went unnoticed by the owner for a couple of years. After a couple years of owner neglect, the boat ended up in a shop for a thorough servicing. The lower unit was removed for inspection and this problem was discovered (along with a quite a few other worn and damaged parts).

With a little care, a few new parts, and a good mechanic (Mau Marine), the lower end and boat were back in service. The old, rusted universal joint was removed and replaced, along with a few shafts, gimbles, bearings, and the leaky bellows. The lower unit will be good for another few years of service.

unit could be attached to the transom of the boat and in close proximity to the engine location. Shorter driveshafts and more compact installations allowed the designers an opportunity to use that open space for owner comfort.

Stern drives were not without their problems. Mounting everything toward the stern of the boat was a balancing headache. It also was a headache developing stern-drive units that could withstand the torque from the engine and the stress of use.

Over 69,300 stern-drive boats are sold annually, and many of the manufacturers have stated that the stern-drive units should be good for about 500 hours or more, which means there are a lot of old drives on boats. At a reasonable estimate of 50 hours per year, that gives the stern-drive boats a lifespan of at least 10 years. If you keep the maintenance up on the unit, it could last even longer!

You should take the boat in for service at least every two years and have a mechanic remove the lower end. There are a couple of things that need to be done that are very difficult for the owner if he or she does not have the experience and the equipment. Over time, the bellow can become damaged, which can allow water to enter the gimble and universal-joint area. This can cause a tremendous amount of rust that will damage the driveshaft, bearings, and splined areas in the lower end.

The lower unit can be removed fairly easily, but it is awkward and difficult to handle for most people. A good shop will have a lift designed for the job and will be able to remove the lower unit in a matter of minutes. After the removal, they can inspect the bellows, gimbles, universal joints, and so forth. While the lower unit is off the boat, they can align the driveshaft to eliminate excessive wear and vibration. Again, this can be done at home in the garage, with the proper training and equipment. However, it's really one of those items that you should let the professionals handle.

PROJECT 22 ★ *Basic Stern-Drive and Outboard Service*

When: Inspect each time you use the boat, and service at least at the beginning and end of season

Time: 2–3 hours

Tools: Flashlight or light; grease gun and grease; sandpaper (320- and 400-grit wet/dry) or emery cloth; fine steel wool; long-handled part-cleaner brush or disposable stiff-bristle paintbrush; masking tape; masking or newspaper; sandpaper; small paint brush or cotton swabs

Supplies: Spray degreaser; acetone or paint thinner; metal primer; touchup paint; metal polish; water; CRC silicone spray; liquid grease-fighting dishwashing soap; paint thinner; aerosol metal primer; marine paste wax; UV-resistant fabric engine cover

Talent: ★★★

Tab: $35–50

Tip: Clean and dry before painting. Do not use any coarse polish or sandpaper on the chrome or stainless lift rods, or it will damage the finish and will not be repairable. Don't skip inspecting the transom, inside and out, at this time. Always clean after any saltwater use

Gain: Safety—the risk of damaged parts or cables

Outboard-motor maintenance starts with a thorough visual inspection of the engine, the mounts, steering and control cables, paint, engine cover condition, and propeller. Servicing the stern drive is the same—start with a visual inspection.

While inspecting, look for loose connections, frayed cables, and anything else that might indicate incorrect adjustments or unusual wear. Often a steering or control cable can slip from its attachment point and begin to bind. Maybe there is sign of a sharp bend, or kink, in the cable that would someday stop the movement or even break the cable and/or housing.

Look for signs of leaks, chips, worn areas, and any visible damage. Locate all the grease zerks (you may need the manufacturer's service manual to get them all), but leave the greasing to last.

When inspecting the outboard mounting brackets, look for loose bolts, brackets, and any signs of movement at the attach points. One nightmare is to hit the throttle, have the engine twist in its mounts, and then either jump from the mount or bind a steering or throttle cable. You don't see it often, but it does happen, and it's really hard to explain to the insurance company that your outboard motor left the transom and jumped into the water by itself.

While you are looking at the mounting brackets, inspect the inside and outside of the transom. This is a good time to look for damage to the transom coating that might jeopardize the strength of the internal structure. Many transoms are wood-laminated, and covered with fiberglass material. If the glass is damaged or cracked, the substructure inside the transom area can become waterlogged and unusable. Waterlogged wood will not only lower the strength of the transom, but it will also add weight to the stern of the boat, creating performance issues.

Inspection of any cable attach points is critical. Control cable ends become dry and need to be regularly lubricated to make sure they work freely. Remove the cable attachments, apply waterproof grease to the connection, and reconnect the cables.

Inspect the exterior of the outboard or lower unit and note any areas that need sanding, primer, and

After inspecting the lower unit, use a spray degreaser to remove the dirt and grime. Dirt and grease can damage hoses and seals, so it's important to keep the unit clean. Most lower units only get a thorough cleaning when they are taken in for service. They should be inspected and cleaned before every use.

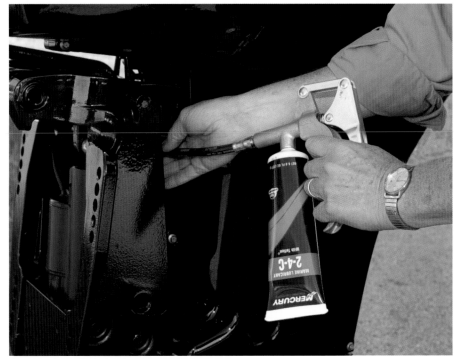

Waterproof grease helps to prevent damage to components from the constant contact with moisture. *Mercury Marine*

touchup paint. Inspect the steering hydraulic cylinder, power tilt cylinders, and any hoses that are attached.

Spray the degreaser on the engine or stern drive and scrub the greasy areas with the stiff-bristle brush to loosen the dirt and grime so it can be washed off. There shouldn't be too much grease and grime on the lower unit itself, but it will be around the mounts and tilt areas or anywhere that grease was used. Rinse the degreasing solution off with freshwater. Power washer is best, but a hose and spray nozzle will do the job.

After overall cleaning of the drive, inspect the steering and trim/tilt hydraulic cylinders. The hydraulic cylinders are very reliable and simple. They will sometimes have corrosion and pitting that can damage the seals, allowing them to leak and not maintain position.

Inspect the exterior of the cylinders for corrosion and pitting, the pushrods for pitting and scratches, and the seals for leaks. You'll also want to look at the hoses for cracking, splitting, and leaks. Don't try to

A lower unit that is covered with a heavy buildup may need to be sanded or acid washed to remove the crud. If there is any damage or corrosion, it should be repaired as soon a possible. If the skeg is nicked or bent, use a file or a Dremel tool with a grinding bit to smooth the damaged area. Small bends can be removed with a rubber mallet, or a small hammer, and a block of wood. Major bends or missing pieces must be repaired by a professional shop.

patch hydraulic hoses. They are under an extreme amount of pressure and if they are cracked or leaking, replace them.

Inspect the polished pushrods. The pushrods are usually stainless or chromed material and any corrosion can create pits in the surface. The pits will cause the seals to wear prematurely and the hydraulic fluid will leak out of the system. Apply a metal polish to the pitted areas and smooth them out. If necessary, use a fine steel wool and polish to remove the corrosion. If the pits and corrosion are extensive, look for replacement parts. Deep gouges will be nothing but problems for the seals and they will require replacement.

Run the tilt up or down a couple of times and inspect the seals for any leakage. If the seals are leaking, they will need to be replaced. The replacement is something probably best left to the local dealer, and it should be done before painting.

Corrosion on the exterior of the hydraulic cylinders can be corrected with sanding and re-painting, just like the rest of the outboard or stern drive. If the corrosion is completely through the paint, it's best to use a metal primer prior to applying a coat of paint.

Sand any damaged area that needs to be re-painted. If bare metal is visible, give the area a good coat of metal primer. This is also a good time to inspect and replace the sacrificial anodes. Check the skeg for any damage. If the skeg has minor nicks and

chips, sand with the sandpaper or emery cloth, and then apply the primer and paint. If the skeg is bent or is missing large pieces, it should be taken to a maintenance facility for repair. Many times a shop will be able to weld additional material onto the skeg to replace the lost pieces, and they can also straighten a bent skeg. Any repairs of that type need to be done by a shop with the correct equipment. Welding or bending can damage the gear case, resulting in costly repairs or replacement of the lower unit.

Typically, you can sand the damaged areas with 320-grit sandpaper to remove the pits and wipe the unit down with a cloth and paint thinner. If there is a large area (like the skeg) that needs sanding, a cordless drill with a sanding pad will quickly remove the old surface. Make sure you do not use very coarse sandpaper on the power sander or you can damage the metal. Many people get carried away with power sanders and remove too much material. You want to remove the corrosion and a layer of paint, not all the metal housing. If you think you can't remove just a small layer, do the sanding by hand.

With masking tape and a few old newspapers, you can protect areas that you do not want painted. Parts like chrome or stainless pushrods, cable ends, or stainless lines need to be protected from any overspray. If you are painting the lower unit near the propeller, it is wise to remove the propeller and tape the shaft to prevent it from getting overspray.

Apply a coat of metal primer. Re-sand the primed areas with 400-grit sandpaper, and clean the unit with a cloth that has been dampened with paint thinner to remove any last traces of dust and dirt. Apply a coat of the manufacturer's touchup paint.

After the paint is dry, remove the masking tape and paper. Spray a light coat of silicone spray on the polished cylinder rods to help lubricate the seals. Dry seals will crack, deform, and eventually leak.

After about every other trip to the lake, remove the hood of your outboard motor (make sure the engine is turned off and cool to the touch) and apply a thin film of silicone spray to the power head. Make sure to use a type of silicone spray that won't damage rubber and plastic. (One of the best sprays recommended by Suzuki Outboard Motors is CRC brand, heavy-duty silicone lubricant, no. 765-1422.) Spraying the silicone will help lubricate any connections or fittings under the hood.

Finally, an application of a quality marine wax will help to seal and protect the finish against the sun and salt.

Most manufacturers also recommend that you store your outboard and stern drive out of the sunlight when possible. Ultraviolet (UV) rays of the sun can fade and damage the paint finish, and deteriorate the exterior plastic and rubber parts. It's always best to store your engine in the shade or under a quality, UV-resistant fabric cover.

The finish of the lower unit can be sanded by hand with 400-grit wet/dry sandpaper and prepared for paint. The Bosch Compact Tough cordless drill/driver with a quick-change 5-inch pad is probably the quickest way to get rid of the buildup and prep the lower unit for paint. I use the 3M Scotch-Brite abrasive pad to sand the flat areas surprisingly fast.

Use a factory color-matched aerosol paint, if possible.
Mercury Marine

PROJECT 23 ★ *Sacrificial Anodes*

When: Check each time you use the boat. Change when they are at the manufacturer's recommended size (usually half of the original size)

Time: 1 hour

Tools: Correct size of combination wrench (or ratchet and socket) for attachment bolts; sandpaper or emery cloth (320-grit or medium)

Supplies: Replacement anodes; metal primer (aerosol or brush); touchup paint (aerosol or brush on); paintbrush

Talent: ★★

Tab: $25 and up (depending on price of anodes)

Tip: Use the service manual to locate all of the anodes; some anodes are behind the propeller

Gain: Reduces corrosion to the engine and associated components

Sacrificial anodes are, as the name implies, sacrificed to corrosion, instead of sacrificing some major part of the engine or drive unit.

Sacrificial anodes are placed in key areas of the outboard engine or the drive unit and are designed to attract corrosive elements before the rest of the engine components. Therefore, they protect the more expensive engine parts (housings, fittings, etc.).

There are numerous shapes and sizes recommended by the manufacturer. Anodes are not just for use in high-corrosion areas such as saltwater. They should be used if you are running your boat in

Anodes come in all shapes, sizes, and locations. These are mounted on the side of an outboard motor.

Occasionally, the anodes will be located under the propeller.

A sacrificial anode is designed to corrode before the metal on the engine or lower unit. This one is doing its job and probably has another season or two left before it needs to be replaced. When they are about half the original size, unbolt the old ones and install the new. The job takes a matter of minutes.

freshwater or saltwater. It is usually recommended that you have zinc anodes if you are running your boat in saltwater and magnesium anodes if you are operating in freshwater.

If you are operating in extraordinarily corrosive saltwater areas, check with your mechanic to see if you should add any additional anodes. He or she will probably recommend adding an extra zinc anode below the waterline of your boat.

The anodes are economical to replace and should be replaced when they have reached a minimum size, as determined by the manufacturer. Typically, that is when they have corroded to about half their original size.

Removing the anodes is nothing more than removing the bolts that attach the anodes to the engine or drive, then removing the actual anodes, and replacing them.

If there is any corrosion or damage to the underlying surface, now is a good time to sand the area with 320-grit sandpaper (or medium emery paper) and touch up the paint. If sanding takes the paint down to the bare metal, apply a light coat of metal primer before applying the paint.

After the touchup paint has dried, install the new anodes and tighten the attachment bolts as recommended by the manufacture.

85

PROJECT 24 ★ *Lower-Unit Oil Change*

When: **Every 25 hours or each season**

Time: **1–2 hours**

Tools: **Clean drain pan; used-oil reclamation container; screwdriver (appropriate size for drain) for removing drain plug and vent plug**

Supplies: **Gear lube in bottle or tubes (or bulk lube unit)**

Talent: ★ ★ ★

Tab: **$20**

Tip: **Make sure the lower unit has been in a full-down position for at least an hour before checking for moisture. Do not drain very much oil initially to look for moisture. Too much oil in the drip pan will cover the moisture and make it difficult to see**

Gain: **Extends life of gears, better lubrication and cooling of gears**

The oil or gear lube is not the only thing that needs to be maintained on the lower end (outboard or stern drive), but it is an important part of the maintenance.

Water is a major concern for lower units. Water is needed to cool the engine and the lower unit, but it does not offer any lubrication properties for the gears. It is good for water to be running through the cooling jackets, but bad to be mixing water with the oil and lubricating the gears.

The first thing to look for is water leaks into the gear case. You'll need to make sure you locate the drain plug. Many an owner has removed a screw from the lower end of the engine only to find that it wasn't the drain plug. Often, it was a screw necessary to hold a clutch or shifting part in place, and if you remove one of those, it means repair-shop time. Use your service manual and make sure you are removing the drain plug. Some lower units have the drain plugs behind the propeller and under the sacrificial anodes. Some plugs are on the side of the lower gear case and some are just ahead of the skeg. Find the right plug first before going any further.

Also find the vent plug, but don't remove it just yet. It's usually located at the top of the lower unit, or about a third of the way up on the outboard lower end.

Put a clean drain pan below the lower unit and remove the drain plug. Without the vent plug removed, the oil (and or water) should just dribble out

(which is what you want). Since water is heavier than oil, it will settle to the bottom of the lower end (beneath the oil) and will be the first thing that drains from the opening.

Always use a drain pan to collect the oil. Not only is this environmentally better, but you need to see what is draining out of the lower end. Replace the lower plug and inspect the drainage. Are water bubbles visible? Does the oil look milky or cloudy? If not, it's a pretty good bet there is no water contamination. If the engine was just run or had recent repairs, the oil may look bubbly or cloudy from the sealers used in the repair or the bubbles from recent use. Running will also mix the oil and water, and it will not be as readily apparent.

Make sure the lower unit has been inactive for a while. This will give the water time to separate from the oil, settle to the bottom, and the bubbles will dissipate. Typically, the lower unit needs to be in a full-down position for at least an hour before checking for moisture.

If there are signs of moisture, it's time to take the unit to a mechanic and have the shop pressure-test the lower unit. Checking with air pressure will help to find the leak and where it is located. The mechanic can take the appropriate repair steps, which will probably include replacing a few seals.

With the drain pan in place, remove the lower plug and the vent plug. This should allow the oil to

Removing the vent plug (the upper plug) should be done after the lower plug has already been removed. If the upper plug is not removed, a vacuum can be created and restrict the drainage of the oil from the lower end.

As the oil drains into a pan, look for signs of moisture or metal filings. There will often be a very small "glitter" look to the oil. The glitter indicates a small amount of metal filings in the oil. Very faint or hardly visible specks are acceptable. Large flecks of metal (like a metal flake paint job) is too much metal. Moisture will typically look like water or a white area in the oil. Water is heavier than oil and the water should dribble out of the drain first. The tan areas are not unusual and do not mean that there is anything wrong with the oil. If there were puddles or bubbles of water, or white foamy areas, then the lower end should probably be pressure-tested by your mechanic.

Bulk refilling units make the job faster. After the oil has drained, insert the nozzle from the bulk pump into the lower drain hole and start pumping the oil into the lower end. If you have a dip stick to measure the level, stop periodically to check it. If not, just wait for the oil level to reach the vent and start draining from the vent.

drain freely from the gear case. If you do this during cold weather without warming the oil it will take forever to drain, if it drains at all.

After all the lubricant has drained from the gear case, it is time to refill. If you have a bulk-style container, it will have enough oil to fill the gear case without changing bottles or tubes. The bulk containers are really handy to use, but not really practical for an owner to have. Usually you find them at the marina shops. If you are one of the lucky owners of a bulk system, you will have a nozzle that you hold firmly into the lower drain hole and you will pump the lever to force the oil into the gear case. As the oil fills the gear case, it will work through the lower unit and toward the vent hole. When the oil starts to dribble out of the vent hole, replace and tighten the vent plug, but don't relax the filler nozzle pressure or the oil will leak back out.

After replacing the vent plug, use one swift movement to remove the filler nozzle and insert the drain plug. Tighten the drain plug, and wipe the area around both plugs to remove any excess oil. Check for leaks, and you are done.

If you don't have the bulk filler tank, the process is basically the same, but you are filling the lower unit with oil from a tube or bottle. One tube will not fill the gear case, so you will have to remove the empty oil tube to insert another fresh tube. That means having the bottles or tubes open and ready to go prior to starting the project. It will also mean plugging the vent while switching tubes. A second person makes this a little easier, but one person can do it.

Drain the oil as before; insert the tube or bottle of oil into the bottom drain and start squeezing the lubricant into the lower end of the engine. When the first tube or bottle of oil is empty, place a finger over the vent hole or replace the vent plug. Quickly remove the empty bottle and insert the nozzle of the new bottle. Remove your finger or the vent plug, and then continue the filling process. Repeat, if necessary. Again, after the oil starts to dribble out of the vent hole, replace the vent plug and then the drain plug. This process works better if you have a couple of extra hands to help open the tubes and pass them to you. If not, get the oil containers open and set up within reach before you start the process.

A few stern drives have a "dip stick" on the end of the vent plug and require checking the oil level with the dip stick instead of when the oil exits the vent. On those units, if the oil exits the vent, it's probably too much. This would be another time when an extra set of hands can help monitor the level.

If your boat has an oil reservoir, you will want to remove it from its mount and clean the sediment from the bottom of the tank. This will require disconnecting the oil line and plugging it with a pencil or similar item. You might need to hold it at a higher level than the tank was mounted. Holding at a higher level will keep the oil in the line from draining out of the line.

Drain the oil in the tank and pour it into a reclamation container for disposal. If you have parts cleaner solution available, you'll need to pour a small amount into the tank, replace the lid, cover the drain fittings, and shake the unit to loosen all the sludge that is in the bottom. After it is cleaned, drain the cleaner from the tank, let it dry, and replace the lines and tank to their original position. Refill to the level as directed by the service manual.

Winterizing the lower end of your outboard or stern drive is really nothing more than following the

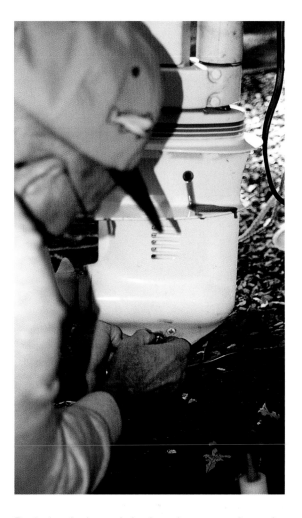

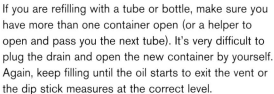

If you are refilling with a tube or bottle, make sure you have more than one container open (or a helper to open and pass you the next tube). It's very difficult to plug the drain and open the new container by yourself. Again, keep filling until the oil starts to exit the vent or the dip stick measures at the correct level.

Replacing the lower drain plug takes an act of speed with your hands. For me, the best way is to plug the vent with your finger, the vent plug, or another person's finger. Then insert the lower drain plug and screw it in tight.

oil-change information. All you are trying to do is make sure there is no water in the gear case before the winter months (and freezing temperatures) arrive. Typically, a lower-end oil change is done at the end of the season. This drains any moisture from the gear case and replaces the old oil with fresh oil. If you have been maintaining your lower end throughout the year (touchup paint, changing the oil, lubricating the prop shaft), make sure you time one of the last servicings just before the winter (at the end of your season) and you should be ready for the winter months.

It's also a good time to replace any sacrificial anodes that are less than half their original size.

If you live in an area that allows you to use the boat throughout the winter, you will need to check for moisture every time you take the boat out of the water and store it. The lower end will not need a complete oil change each time, but you will need to drain oil to look for and remove water (and then top the lower end off with new oil).

PROJECT 25 ★ *Minor Propeller Repairs*

When: Each time you take the boat out, or at least the beginning and end of season

Time: 1 hour

Tools: Aluminum file; small rubber mallet; ball-peen hammer; 2x4x8-inch piece of scrap wood (pine or oak, depending on necessary bend); sandbag; 320-grit sandpaper; manufacturer touchup paint; prop-shaft grease as recommended by the manufacturer

Talent: ★ ★ ★

Tab: $15

Tip: Do not try to straighten sharp bends. Take it to a shop

Gain: Bent and chipped propellers reduce the amount of thrust they can produce, reducing performance

While it seems like the propeller is a very small part of the boat, without it, you aren't going anywhere. If the propeller is damaged, it damages the rest of the engine, and that fact alone makes it a critical component.

So while it is small, it is something that needs to be maintained and checked on a regular basis. Every time you take the boat out of the water (or after a spin on the lake if you keep it on a lift), you should inspect the propeller. Look for nicks, chips, and bends. You

Rocks, sand, and logs can really damage a propeller. Damaged propellers cannot move the water as efficiently or as smoothly, therefore reducing performance and efficiency. And not only that, it can damage the lower-end components.

Many smaller nicks can be removed with a hand file. Another method is to use the cordless Dremel with a grinder bit to remove chips and smooth out nicks. Be careful not to remove too much material from the blades, or the propeller may need to be rebalanced.

Most propellers will slide on the shaft freely. If yours is stubborn, you may need to lightly tap the propeller with a mallet to "break" it loose.

By using the cordless drill/driver with a sanding or grinding pad, you can sand the rough areas and smooth the finish in preparation for painting.

The advantage of the cordless Dremel is its size. The Dremel bits are able to get into the small areas of the propeller, removing corrosion and old paint.

will also want to look for line or rope wrapped around the shaft and under the propeller. Any line of rope can damage the seals and wear the prop shaft.

There are a few basic guidelines for an owner to follow. Stainless steel propellers, severely damaged propellers, and adjustable pitch propellers should be sent to a specialized propeller repair facility. A "prop" shop will have the appropriate equipment to repair, refinish, and rebalance the propeller for the best performance. Remember, they usually do not do these repairs overnight, so always keep a backup propeller to use while one is being repaired.

For aluminum propellers with minor dings, nicks, or bends, an owner can do some very limited maintenance. Typically, these are just minor cosmetic repairs. The propeller needs to be smooth and in good condition to provide the boat with maximum performance. Nicks and bends reduce the efficiency, so it's logical to check them after every use and make minor repairs when necessary.

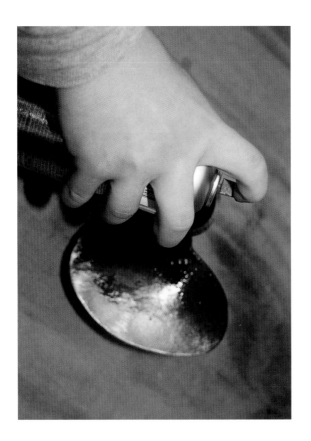

Place the propeller on a clean, flat surface. Make sure it is not near anything that will be damaged by the overspray. Spray even coats of paint on the propeller, and hold the aerosol can or paint gun about 5 to 8 inches from the propeller as you are spraying. Move the spray in smooth strokes. Do not stop moving without stopping the spray. Too much paint in one area will cause runs or drips.

Also, you should periodically remove the propeller and apply a film of grease to the propeller shaft. Why not repair the propeller at the same time?

While the propeller is still *on* the engine, it is a great time to file any nicks or chips out of the prop. Use a small aluminum file to smooth the damaged area. You do not want to remove a lot of material; all you need to do is smooth the area so there are not sharp or jagged edges.

If the nick is in a location that appears to be bent, remove the propeller before filing. With a rubber mallet and a bag of sand (like the ones you can buy to add weight in the back of your pickup truck), you can remove the bend in the blade. Place the blade against the sandbag and use the mallet to hammer the bend back into alignment. If the sandbag is not firm enough, try a block of wood. Oak or another hard wood offers a very firm backing surface. Pine is soft and will behave more like a sandbag. The type of backing material will depend on how difficult the bend is to remove.

If the rubber mallet doesn't remove the bend, you can use a ball-peen hammer. Be careful, abuse of the ball-peen hammer can result in damage to the blades of the propeller that will be worse than leaving the bend in the blade.

If the blade has a sharp bend, send it to a prop shop. Straightening sharp bends can harden the metal and cause it to crack or weaken. Don't take a chance that the propeller throws a blade. The resulting vibration from the out of balance propeller can twist the shaft, ruin the seals, and destroy the gears.

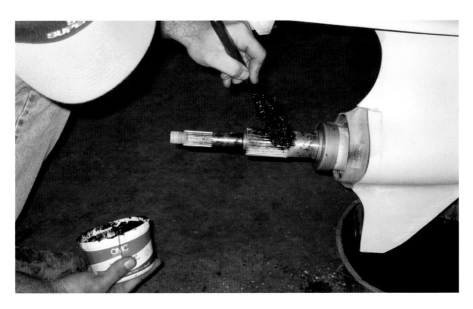

One way to help prevent damage to the propeller shaft is to apply an appropriate waterproof grease prior to installing the propeller.

SECTION 5

WINTERIZING AND STORING

Projects 26 through 36

Winterizing your boat can be once a year or multiple times per year. It depends on your location and how you use the boat. Regardless, winterization should be looked at as regular maintenance. In fact, a full winterization boils down to performing the maintenance in this book, plus a couple of additional projects.

Winterization includes addressing the oil and filters; belts and hoses; the exterior and interior; the engine and drive unit, or outboard exterior care.

Winterizing is more than just taking care of the boat. If you keep your boat on a lift, it too needs to be ready for the long, cold season. Removing covers, greasing pulleys and fittings, and repairing damage are all part of winterizing.

This can be a scene after every use, or once a year. If it's the last trip of the season, this might be a good time to do the fogging of the engine or add the fuel stabilizer.

Review those areas and add a few additional projects such as tending to cabin accessories and the fuel, adding antifreeze, and shrink-wrapping the boat. You should also winterize the trailer before placing it in storage.

If you decide to take your boat to a shop for winterization, they will usually complete the following types of services. Many of the shops figure that this might be the only time that the boat gets these items serviced, so they offer it as a winterization package. If you have already been doing these service items, the winterization can be reduced to just a few vital areas such as fuel, lubrication, and removal of water or treatment of the cooling system. The following checklist is a helpful guide to winterization.

- Run the motor. Check the timing and basic operations.
- Drain and inspect the lower-unit gear lube, and refill with it manufacturer's recommended gear lube.
- Add fuel stabilizer to preserve both the fuel and the fuel tank for the upcoming winter and spring months.
- Apply anti-corrosion grease to all fittings, linkages, and steering cables.
- Inspect the throttle, steering, and shift cables for binding and wear.
- Inspect the water-pump housing and impeller.
- Inspect the lower-unit seals and pressure-check it if necessary.
- Drain water from the block and manifolds, and re-fill with marine-grade antifreeze.
- Drain oil from the engine, refill with the manufacturer's recommended oil, and replace the oil filter.
- On four-stroke models, change the oil filter and refill with manufacturer's recommended four-stroke oil.
- Replace water-separator filter.
- Fog the engine block, carburetors, and fuel lines.
- Grease all other fittings and steering cables with marine-grade grease.
- Check all belts, hoses, and the general condition of the boat motor, drive, and lower unit.

PROJECT 26 ★ *Fuel System Winterizing and Storing*

When: Each time you take the boat out, or at least the beginning and end of season

Time: 1–2 hours

Tools: Earmuff flush adapter; hose

Supplies: Fuel stabilizer (additive like ValvTect Marine Gasoline and Diesel Stabilizer or Sta-Bil); ValvTect Marine Premium Fogging Oil; and pressure wate

Talent: ★ ★ ★

Tab: $35

Tip: Make sure all other service work that requires the engine to be running is completed prior to fogging the engine

Gain: Faster and trouble-free start-up next year

When fuel is being stored for a period of time, the chemical structure can break down. It gets old. When fuel gets old it will clog up the engine, burn inconsistently, and be a problem to use (plus it stinks!). You have two options: Remove the fuel or treat the fuel with a fuel stabilizer. Most people opt for treating the fuel. Removing the fuel would mean getting all the fuel out of the tank and lines to leave the fuel tank empty. Leaving a fuel tank empty might or might not be a problem, depending on the type of material it is made from and the location of the storage. If you leave it empty, condensation can build up in the tank. If it is a steel tank, being empty leaves the metal uncovered and susceptible to corrosion. If the tank has a rubber type of liner (bladder), the rubber liner will dry out and give way to cracks and leaks.

Leave the fuel tank filled with fuel, but treated with a fuel additive like ValvTect or Sta-Bil. These fuel additives will increase the longevity of the fuel's composition, preventing it from breaking down. Hopefully, when you take the boat out of storage the

If you plan on leaving your boat for any length of time, fill the tank and put fuel stabilizer in the fuel. ValvTect Marine Fuel Stabilizer helps keep the fuel's integrity by reducing sludge, glazing, and gunk. Run the engine long enough to get the treated fuel throughout the fuel lines, pump, and carburetor.

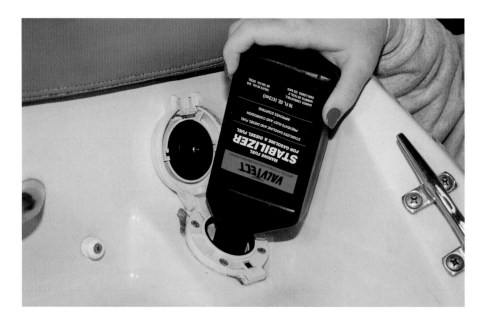

When the engine is just about done running the treated fuel through the system, start spraying fogging oil into the carburetor or intake of the engine. Follow the manufacturer's instructions, but you will want the engine to start smoking and running rough before you shut it off and stop spraying the fogging oil. Fogging oil is delivered into the engine to coat the internal components and reduce the risk of damage from corrosion while the boat is being parked for an extended period of time.

following season, the fuel will still be good for that first trip on the water. If you are running a diesel engine, you should also look into something to prevent bacteria and fungi from growing in the diesel fuel. ValvTect makes BioGuard Fuel Micro-biocide. The biggest disadvantage of leaving the boat full of fuel is safety; a tank full of fuel is a potential fire hazard.

After treating the supply in the fuel tank, you will need to get the treated fuel through the lines and into the engine. This is the time to drain and/or replace the fuel-water separator filter. Next, start the engine and let it run to ensure that the treated fuel reaches the fuel lines (approximately 15 minutes).

At the same time, we need to get the inside of the engine lubricated for storage. Just parking the boat puts the internal components at risk of corrosion, especially the cylinder walls, camshaft, and crankshaft. Fogging oil sticks on the internal parts of the engine. The consistency is thicker and stickier than regular oil, and it has additives that can help reduce or prevent corrosion. To utilize fogging oil, run the engine and spray fogging oil into the cylinders until the engine stalls. The fogging oil is then taken into the engine to coat the internal parts, thereby protecting the inside parts from corrosion. To do this, attach a can of fogging oil to the fitting on the intake, or spray it directly into the carburetor after removing the air filter.

Fogging the inside can also be done manually. First, remove the spark plug(s) and the stop-switch lanyard cord from your outboard. This is also a good

time to make sure the spark plug wires are off the spark plugs to prevent starting. If you have a manual-start engine, use the starter rope to slowly turn the engine over while spraying the storage oil into the spark plug holes. You can also spray fogging oil into the carburetor while turning the engine over.

If you have an electric-start engine, spray the fogging oil into the spark plug holes, and using the electric starter, turn the engine over in short bursts. Do not continually run the starter or it could cause damage to the starter. It's also a very good idea to have a flush kit hooked up to your water intakes (before turning over the engine) to prevent damage to the engine's water pump. Again, spraying into the carburetor can send the fogging oil through the carburetor and into the intake system.

Never run your engine without cooling water attached through an earmuff-style flush adapter or a permanent flushing adapter. You can run the fuel through the system and apply the fogging oil while the boat is in the water, just before you take it out for storage.

Also, remember to disconnect the battery and remove it. Store the battery in a warm, dry area in your garage or basement. Removing the battery will remove any source of spark, ignition, or heat that might be caused by a short or damaged electrical component. Store your battery fully charged and on a block of wood. Do not leave the battery sitting on concrete. If the battery is charged, the electrolyte and water should not freeze. If the battery is low on charge, there is a greater chance of freezing.

PROJECT 27 ★ *Cooling System Winterizing and Storing*

When: Each time you take the boat out, or at least the beginning and end of season

Time: 1–2 hours

Tools: Jack or dolly to lift front of boat; flush adapter (earmuff-style); hose and water; StarBrite Do It Yourself Winterizing Kit; combination wrench or sockets to fit drain plugs

Supplies: Antifreeze (ethylene glycol for the closed system; propylene glycol for a raw-water system)

Talent: ★★★★

Tab: $75–100

Tip: If you are not confident that you can remove all the water from the system, do not attempt this procedure

Gain: Prevents damage from corrosion and freezing over the winter

Raise the front of the boat with the dolly, or in this case, with a floor jack. Elevating the front will drain all the moisture to the back of the boat. Open all of the drain valves on your engine. Make sure you use the service manual and do not miss any of the drains. Any moisture left in the engine can cause severe damage.

Any fluids left in the boat have the potential to freeze and cause damage. The boat needs to be drained of all fluids, or the fluids need to be mixed with the appropriate type of antifreeze to prevent the water from freezing.

The best thing to do is to raise the front of the boat. Raise the boat by cranking the trailer dolly up, putting a jack under the frame, or attaching it to the tow vehicle. Whatever the method, you need to get the bow in the air so the water will drain out of the transom drain.

If you haven't already done this, backwash the cooling system and lower unit to get rid of salt, sediment, and rust flakes. If not, get out the earmuff-style flushing kit that clamps onto the water intake and review the fuel storage section. Some of the newer drive units and outboards actually have a factory-installed flushing attachment point.

Most mechanics agree that after flushing the system, all of the drain plugs will need to be removed from the engine block, manifolds, water pumps, and coolers. Many of the newer engines have brightly colored drain plugsthat are removable by hand. Older models will need an appropriate combination wrench to remove them. You will need a service manual to locate all of the drain plugs. You do not want to miss

Close all of the drains on the engine. Install the earmuff flush adapter to the lower-end water intake ports. Run the engine long enough to open the thermostat (if you have one). Shut off the engine and remove the garden hose and water supply. Connect the winterizing kit to the flush adapter. StarBrite's winterizing kit consists of a 5-gallon plastic container that you put the antifreeze in and a valve and hose to connect to the flush adapter. Turn the antifreeze container valve on, allowing the antifreeze to be drawn into the engine through the flush adapter. Start the engine and let it idle. When the antifreeze flows through the engine and exits the exhaust and propeller, shut off the engine. Tilt the lower end up, then disconnect the flush kit and antifreeze. *Star Brite*

any drain plugs and risk leaving any water in the system to freeze. Freezing can crack the block or manifold.

Draining takes place whether you have a full raw-water system or you have a closed-water system. Raw water systems use seawater that is pumped through the system for cooling. The closed system will have a portion of the system that is self-contained or closed off from the seawater. This system has a storage tank and pumps water through the cooling jackets and heat exchanger, much like the cooling system on an automobile (minus the radiator). Some large engines have a closed system and radiator, just like an auto.

A closed system needs to have the appropriate mixture of ethylene glycol (antifreeze) and water. Like your car, the mixture should be 50/50. The ethylene glycol helps to transfer heat, reduce corrosion, and prevent freezing. But ethylene glycol is a poison and cannot be drained on the ground or in the water. Care needs to be taken when working with ethylene glycol.

Replace or close all of the drain plugs before filling the system with antifreeze.

Attach the StarBrite winterization kit per the manufacturer's instructions to pull antifreeze into the cooling system. The kit includes a five-gallon plastic container, an adapter, and a hose. The winterization kit's hose attaches to the flushing adapter (earmuff or factory-installed). The plastic container should be placed on a surface higher than the flush adapter (like the swim platform or transom area of the boat). Many of the mechanics use a pink-colored propylene glycol (nontoxic RV antifreeze), which should be good to minus 50 degrees. If you are in an area that requires more protection, you can use a minus 100 degees antifreeze (blue) or a minus 200 degrees antifreeze (blue green). In most cases the pink, minus 50, will do the job.

Turn the valve on the StarBrite plastic container. Start the engine, run at idle, and the cooling system will pull the antifreeze from the container into the engine and its associated components. Make sure that the antifreeze completely fills the engine block, manifold, circulating pump, and so on. Do not shut the engine or antifreeze off until the fluid exiting the engine is the correct color and strength. If necessary, test the antifreeze amount with the appropriate antifreeze tester.

If there is any doubt, check a few drain plugs or valves to make sure antifreeze drains out. If all of this seems too difficult, take it to a shop and let it be done professionally. The risk of expensive repairs is high if the antifreeze is not fully distributed through the system.

It's possible to combine a couple of winterizing projects together at the same time. Add the fuel additive and run the engine in preparation for the antifreeze. Then you can run the antifreeze through the system. When the system has all the antifreeze in it, start spraying the fogging oil. By the time you shut the engine down, the winterizing (antifreeze, fogging, and fuel systems) is all complete at the same time. It might take an extra person or two to do it right the first couple of times.

PROJECT 28 ★ *Cabin Winterizing and Storing*

When: Each time you leave your boat for an extended period of time, or at the end of the season

Time: 2 hours

Tools: Small, plastic dishes to put baking soda in; wet/dry vacuum

Supplies: Moisture-absorption packets; mothballs/crystals; baking soda; white vinegar; water; mild detergent; fabric glue; Scotch Guard

Talent: ★ ★

Tab: $25

Tip: Make sure the carpets are dry before sealing the boat with shrink-wrap or a tarp. Try fabric glue and patch first, then use thread as backup. If the cover can be removed and you have access to a sewing machine, zigzag stitching is the best method of repair

Gain: Helps reduce or prevent rodent and moisture damage over the storage period

Basic cabin care includes not only the cleaning, but also tasks like removing food, controlling mildew, and catching rodents. Before you start cleaning out all the canned goods, take a look at the cushions and pads; this is a great time to patch any tears you might find in the fabric. Patching the fabric when it gets small tears will make it last longer and look better, while protecting the padding material inside.

For fabric repairs you'll need a small, curved needle and thread that matches the fabric; a small piece of fabric; and a small tube of fabric glue or Superglue. Fabric glue is available from most craft or sewing stores (including Wal-Mart). Not all repairs will need a piece of fabric, but if there is a hole that needs to be patched, you will want to put a small reinforcement under the tear. Any similar fabric will do to add the strength, but if you look for a little extra fabric on the inside of the cushion or under the seats, the match will be better. Often there will be enough leftover material under the seat or on a seam inside the cushion to cut a patch.

Cut a small patch from the leftover material that is just a little bigger than the tear. If you are patching a zippered cushion, you should be able to remove the stuffing material and turn the cover inside out. This would allow you to glue the fabric patch directly over the tear and let it cure, possibly with a weight on the area. If the patch is in an area that you can't get to the backside, you'll need to insert the patch material

through the tear, insert the nozzle of the glue around the edges of the tear, and patch. In this case, a little stitching can help hold the patch in place. If you're really good with a needle and thread, you might not even need the glue (I like both, because I'm lousy with a needle and thread). A curved needle is a requirement when working on a tear from one side. You'll want to make small, looped stitches around the edge of the patch and even through the tear. The thread needs to be knotted on the underside of the tear so that it does not show from the top. If you are trying to repair a small tear or pulled seam, you can use the curved needle and thread to overstitch the area with small chain or loop stitches.

Once the glue has cured and the stitching is done, spray the area with a fabric protector like Scotch Guard.

Always remember to remove any food or drink from the boat. Don't leave items that will invite mildew and rodents to your boat. It's also important to remove charts, linens, and electronics and store them in a cool, dry location. Anything that can be damaged by moisture and freezing temperatures should be removed and stored in your basement (or garage, storage unit, etc.). If you have any electrical devices (radios, GPS, loran, etc.) that have batteries, remove the batteries before storing the units. Dry cell batteries have a habit of leaking over time and will damage the unit. By next season, you will need to replace the batteries anyway. Take out the old ones and use them in something else.

101

Most cabins are filled with items in the cabinets and storage areas. Make sure you remove anything that can be damaged and put the items in a dry, cool storage space. Don't leave anything edible in the cabin or you will get bugs and rodents living onboard. *Bill Fedorko*

After cleaning and repairing, remove the interior cushions and jump seats. Store them in a cool, dry place (if possible). If you do not have a place for all the cushions, you will need to store them on end to allow for maximum ventilation. Air circulation will help reduce the spots that will collect moisture.

After removing all of the items from the cabinets and cabin, it's a good idea to run a vacuum through the boat one last time to pick up any dirt or food particles that might attract rodents.

Place mildew-control devices (absorption packets) in a couple of locations in the cabin and also place them in any enclosed lockers or compartments. They are designed to absorb the moisture, which will reduce the mildew, mold, and corrosion in the cabin. You can also place small containers of baking soda around the cabin and in the cabinets to help absorb moisture and odors. If you have a refrigerator or icebox onboard, leave the door open and make sure the interior has been cleaned with antibacterial soap or vinegar and a mild detergent.

You can also place mothballs/crystals around the cabin and in the cabinets to help keep rodents and moths away.

If your boat has any type of freshwater system, you will need to remove the water so it does not freeze. Depending on your boat, you will need to winterize the head, holding tank, and freshwater system. Always try to do any maintenance according to owner's manuals.

There are a couple of ways to winterize the freshwater system. You can add nontoxic antifreeze to the system. You do this by filling the tanks with the correct mixture of antifreeze and start turning on the taps throughout the cabin. Make sure that you turn on only one tap at a time until the antifreeze-colored water flows out of that tap. Then turn that tap off. You will need to repeat this process with every tap in the system (sink, shower, etc). The other option is to drain the freshwater system of all the water. That means you need to open all the drains and taps to let the tank run completely dry. You will also need to disconnect the water lines at the freshwater pump, and all the other water lines at their lowest points so that any moisture left in the system is drained out. It is also a good idea to force the water out of the lines by using compressed air. Don't forget to drain the shower sump and hot-water heater.

PROJECT 29 ★ *Boat Storage*

When: End of season or storage for an extended period of time

Time: 1 hour

Tools: Heat gun or Dr. Shrink propane heat torch

Supplies: Boat shrink-wrap or tarp; tarp tie-downs

Talent: ★★

Tab: $75–250, depending on the tarp or shrink-wrap cost

Tip: If stored outside with a tarp or shrink-wrap, make sure the tarp or shrink-wrap is supported inside the boat so water will not collect. Dr. Shrink's shrink-wrap kit can help

Gain: Protects the finish and material from aging and damage

Before storing, it doesn't hurt to give the finish a nice coat of wax. That will usually prevent stains and spots from sticking to the finish.

After you have cleaned, mothballed, and otherwise completed the preparation to store your boat, where do you store it? If possible, store your boat in a garage. Of course, a temperature-controlled facility is the best. But, if that's not available, the next step is to cover the boat with shrink-wrap or a large tarp. Shrink-wrap is a great way to seal the boat from the outside elements. However, it also seals in the moisture. If you shrink-wrap, make sure you scatter

Shrink wrap seals the boat from the outside elements, but it can also trap the moisture inside. Make sure you have a plan for moisture absorption.

Block the wheels if you can't raise them off the ground. You don't want your boat rolling around unexpectedly and bumping around in the storage facility.

moisture absorption packets around the inside. Damp Rid is a product that you can buy on the Internet or at home stores. It is a container filled with absorption pellets. The pellets are available separately, and are replaced after time when they start to get full of moisture.

Now the bad news. If you shrink-wrap the boat, you will need to clean the areas where the tape sticks with rubbing alcohol. The dirt, wax, and cleaners will have to be removed so the tape can get a good bond. If the tape doesn't stick, when the shrink-wrap starts to shrink it will pull the tape loose and be ineffective. You might think about that before the final coat of wax is put on the boat; leave a strip wax-free where the tape is going to be.

Dr. Shrink provides shrink-wrap kits for all boat sizes (and anything else for that matter), and the kits come with everything you'll need. You will need the shrink-wrap to be big enough for your boat, cords to attach, vents to let air in and out, tape to attach it to the boat, and then a way to shrink it. Shrinking requires heat from a large torch or a big heat gun. Dr. Shrink can send you the torch. Attach it to a propane tank and you are set to shrink. If you need to get in and out of the boat, the company even offers an optional zippered area. If you are stuck in an area where you need to wrap your boat for an extended period of time, check out the full kit for the first year. Then all

you need to do is buy the shrink-wrap material for your size of boat.

If your boat is going to be stored on a trailer, block the wheels of the trailer so they are off the ground and loosen the tie-down straps that are holding the boat in place. Loosening the straps will help to reduce the stress on the hull.

Many people leave their skis, ropes, and inflatable tubes in the boat during storage. That's okay, but make sure they are dry and positioned for maximum airflow to reduce corrosion and mildew. Make sure the ropes are loosely coiled and the bindings on skis and boards are dry. A coat of wax on a ski's or board's finish will help to protect the finish. If there are any metal fittings or skeg, make sure they get coated with a metal polish and protector, or at least a coat of wax.

If possible, do not leave the inflatable stuff in your boat. Store all the inflatable toys in a location that is protected from rodents. Rats, mice, and squirrels like Hypalon and PVC fabrics. Also, do not leave the inflatables exposed to the elements—clouds do not inhibit UV rays.

Again, any time you are planning to leave your boat alone for an extended period of time (over the winter or just storage), it's a good idea to remove the battery and store it in a safe, dry place. Check battery fluid levels and make sure it is fully charged.

PROJECT 30 ★ *Trailer Care*

When: Each time you take the boat out, or at least the beginning and end of season

Time: 1–3 hours, depending on condition of trailer

Tools: Long-handle parts cleaning brush; water hose, spray, nozzle, and water; cordless drill; wire brush for the drill; 320-grit sandpaper; sanding pad; cloth; 2-inch-wide masking tape

Supplies: Spray degreaser; paint thinner; rust primer/sealer; metal rustproof primer; rustproof touchup paint; spray lubricant (WD-40 or silicone spray)

Talent: ★★

Tab: $50

Tip: The best time to do trailer repair is when the boat is in the water. Before unloading the boat, stand behind the trailer and see if one side is lower than the other side. This is usually an indication of a problem

Gain: Repairing rust prevents further damage to trailer, extending life

If you trailer your boat back and forth to the lake, make sure you give it a good visual inspection before each trip to look for chipped paint, rusted spots, frayed light wires, leaky hoses, or worn areas. Of course, the best time to repair anything you find on an inspection is when the boat is off the trailer.

Before you take off with your pride and joy trailing behind your tow vehicle, take a good look at the suspension of the trailer. The suspension absorbs all the bumps, potholes, and other obstacles that are in the road. Inspect the suspension, looking at the shackles for loose bolts, bent shackles, weak springs,

Any chips or rusted areas in the trailer frame should be sanded and treated to prevent further damage. Using a Bosch cordless drill/driver with a wire brush or a scratch pad can remove the loose rust or paint. Then sand the area so it can be primed and painted.

Priming the area with a rust remover is one of the easiest and fastest ways to stop the rust. The rust-remover spray dissolves the existing rust and changes it to a hard material that can be painted over. It also seals the surface and reduces the chances for the area to rust again.

and leaking or weak shocks. If all looks okay, take off for the lake.

The rest of the trailer inspection happens when you put the boat in the water and leave it at the marina slip. That gives you time to take the trailer home for the touchup and repairs. If you don't leave your boat at a slip for the season and you trailer it regularly, the best time for repairs and maintenance is still when the boat is in the water. Tie it up at the dock and go back to work on the trailer. If you are going to do a few repairs while the boat is at the lake, you probably don't have a lot of time, so plan ahead.

If trailer repair is planned, don't plan a big day of boating activities. What you need is the boat tied to a dock for a couple of hours. Pick a warm, not hot, day for repairs and find a place that has a little room in the parking lot. You might want to send the family or friends off in the boat while you tackle the minor trailer repairs.

Inspect the frame and look for chipped paint and rust. Really small spots can be sanded with a sand pad or sandpaper and touched up with a small

paintbrush (I've even used fingernail polish and modeler's paint).

If you find large spots or any small spots that are down to the metal, use your cordless drill and a wire brush attachment to brush the spots so they are free of the loose rust flakes and powder. If you own an aluminum trailer, you will be looking for chips in the paint and corrosion from salt.

Sand the chip or rusted spot (and an area of about 2 inches around the spots) with 320-grit wet/dry sandpaper, or a medium-coarse sanding pad. The sanding pads are pretty handy to use. Most are available in coarse, medium, and fine. The pad material is attached to a handle and that allows a firm grip for scuffing up an area on the trailer frame.

After sanding, use a clean cloth and paint thinner to remove the sanding dust and any wax, grease, or dirt.

With the aerosol can of rustproof metal primer, prime the area carefully. You might want to use 2-inch-wide masking tape and tape an area of about 3 inches around the chipped or rusted area to prevent overspray to the rest of the trailer, rollers, or pads.

WD-40 or spray silicone will keep the rollers turning freely and help prevent the shaft from getting corroded.

Most hardware and auto supply stores now sell a spray that is designed to stop the rust and seal/prime it for a coat of paint. Usually it turns the rusted area a dark, black color. With this spray, the directions require removing loose rust and flakes with a wire brush or by sanding it, but you do not have to take the area down to bare metal. This process is probably best when you are working under time constraints.

After the rust sealer or primer is dry, follow the directions to coat with a color-matched manufacturer's touchup paint. Always touch up using rust-proof paint. The trailer goes in and out of the water and gets hit with rocks from the road. It's susceptible to lots of little nicks, chips, and scratches.

Depending on your fenders, when you back the trailer into the water to load or unload the boat, run a brush under the fender to make sure to knock any mud or grime off the bottom sides. If the fenders are very close to the tires, you may have to wait until you remove the tire to clean under the fender.

Check the bumpers and rollers for missing pieces of carpet or rubber. Make sure there are not any foreign objects embedded in the roller or bumper surface that can scratch or damage the boat hull during loading and transportation.

Use a spray lubricant like WD-40 or a silicone spray to lubricate the rollers and the winch. If the winch is really dry, you may want to apply a little bit of waterproof grease to the shaft and the locking mechanism.

PROJECT 31 ★ *Wheel and Tire Removal*

When: Inspect each time you take the boat out; repair at least at the beginning and end of season, or when winterizing

Time: 1–2 hours

Tools: Hose; water and nozzle; scrub brush; lug wrench or ratchet; socket and extension; jack and jack stand

Supplies: Spray degreaser; water; parts-cleaner solution

Talent: ★ ★ ★

Tab: $10

Tip: Make sure you block the opposite wheels and the jack stand to prevent the trailer from moving

Gain: Access to hub and brake drum (if equipped), allows you to inspect springs and shocks

The wheels and tires of the trailer should be inspected every time you go for a drive. Just like your car, you should make sure that the tires have the correct air pressure, do not show any signs of damage, and have ample tread. That inspection should be done each and every trip. It is also very important that you flush the brakes and wheels after saltwater use to prevent corrosion and damage. Just use a hose and freshwater to rinse the wheels, tire hubs, and the brake assembly. You may need to spray the backside of the brake drum with water to flush the internal parts.

If your trailer has brakes, you will need to do a few additional things when you have removed the hub. Make sure you clean and service the brake drum per the factory recommendations. This should include cleaning and lubricating the springs and fittings, but not the brake shoes. You will also need to inspect the brake shoes and clean as recommended by the factory.

At least once a year, and usually at the start and the end of the season, the wheel hubs and bearings need a little more care. When you back the trailer into the water; the tires, wheels, and hubs are submerged. If there is any leakage into the hub, the water could corrode and pit the bearings. Pits in the bearings can cause them to fail while you are pulling the trailer down the freeway on vacation. A stuck bearing could cause the loss of a tire and wheel, or create a skidding,

out-of-control trailer. The bearings need to be inspected for damage and packed with grease. One way to reduce the risk of moisture damage (corrosion) to the bearings is to keep the hubs filled with waterproof grease. To do that, you need to repack the bearings and hub (at least once a year). You can purchase caps for the wheel hub that have a grease zerk installed in them. These caps allow you to pump grease into the hub and help keep the water out. The downside is that if you pack them too full of grease, you can damage the seals. Too much grease can force the grease out of the seals and make it easier for the water to get into the hub.

Start by cleaning the wheel, hub, and lug nuts or bolts. Spray degreaser onto the hub or center area of the wheel. With a stiff-bristle scrub brush, loosen the grease and grime and then rinse the wheel and hub clean. After it's clean, put a block of wood or brick in front of and behind both tires. This will keep the trailer from rolling while you are working on the tire and wheel.

Place the jack under the axle (if possible), or under a spot on the fame close to the axle and close to the tire you are going to remove. If necessary, add blocks of wood as spacers between the jack and frame.

Loosen all of the wheel lug nuts with the appropriate lug wrench or a ratchet and socket. Do not take them out completely, just loosen them slightly.

Spraying degreaser on the hub and lug nuts of the trailer not only makes it look better, but it makes it easier to work on. Dirt and grease can also be a safety hazard. The lug wrench could slip off the lug nuts, causing injury.

Lug wrenches or a socket, extension, and a ratchet can be used to remove the lug bolts. Most lugs will take at least a ½-inch drive ratchet to get enough leverage to loosen the lugs. Make sure you get the correct lug wrench for the size of lugs on your trailer. If you damage or round the lugs, it will make it a lot more difficult, not to mention expensive, to remove.

Using the jack, lift the trailer high enough so that the tire and wheel just clear the ground and can spin freely. As a safety precaution, place the jack stand under the frame to prevent the trailer from falling if it slips off the jack.

Fill the small can or bucket with parts-cleaner solution. This is where you will place all of the bearing parts to be cleaned before filling them with new grease (see Project 32).

When the wheel is free to turn, remove the lug nuts/bolts and remove the tire and wheel as well. Set the tire and wheel assembly aside.

PROJECT 32 ★ *Hub and Bearing Cleaning*

When: Inspect each time you take the boat out, repair when winterizing or at least at the beginning and end of season

Time: 2–3 hours

Tools: Flat screwdriver; small hammer or mallet; large pliers; wooden dowel (a few inches longer than the depth of the hub); small metal can for soaking small parts; clean cloth

Supplies: Waterproof wheel-bearing grease; parts-cleaning solvent (paint thinner works)

Talent: ★ ★ ★

Tab: $75–$100

Tip: When removing the bearing cap, do not bend or damage it with the sharp edge of the screwdriver

Gain: An opportunity to inspect the hub, bearings, and races for condition

Using the screwdriver, pry the cap out of the hub. There is usually a small lip to pry against. You might need to use the hammer or mallet to tap the screwdriver's blade between the lip on the cap and the hub.

As you remove the parts, starting with the cap, place them in the parts-cleaner bucket. Under the cap will be a slotted hex nut with a cotter pin. The cotter pin is inserted in the slots in the nut and passed through the axle to prevent the nut from loosening. The cotter pin has the straight ends bent over the end of the axle to prevent it from sliding out of the hole.

With a pair of pliers, straighten the pin and remove it carefully from the nut and axle.

Remove the nut. This might require help from the pliers, but it probably will not. Many end up being

Use a small-tipped chisel or flat-bladed screwdriver to pry the edge of the hubcap from the hub. Work your way around the cap until it can be removed from the hub and place it in the cleaning solution.

Remove the cotter key from the nut and loosen the nut. After the nut is removed, place it in a parts-cleaning solution or acetone.

Using a small can (an old coffee can in this picture) or a parts-cleaner tub, clean the bearings, nut, caps, and associated parts with parts-cleaner solution or acetone. Paint thinner also works. An old paintbrush can be used to scrub the parts and remove any residue.

finger-tight and can be removed with just a slight amount of pressure.

Keep track of the sequence of the parts that you remove. Under the nut should be a washer and the outside bearing. All of these items should be removed and placed in the cleaner.

Pull the hub from the axle and place it facedown on a clean piece of wood, paper, cardboard, or cloth. The inside bearing is held in place by the seal. The seal needs to be removed first. Typically, if you are going this far to clean the bearings, you should replace the seals. In that case, use the screwdriver to pry the old seal out of the hub since you have no need to reuse it. If you need to keep the seal, you will need to insert a wooden dowel (or scrap wood) through the hub from the lug nut/bolt side and tap the seal from inside the hub. After the seal has been removed, next remove the bearing and place it in the parts cleaner.

While the bearings are soaking in the solvent, use extra solvent and the brush to clean the inside of the hub and the metal that the bearing rubs against (races). The races should be smooth and free of worn areas. If they have any damage, they will need to be replaced.

Clean the parts using the stiff-bristle brush (parts-cleaner brushes work the best), remove the parts and place them on a clean cloth or rag to dry. Compressed air is helpful to remove the solvent from the internal areas of the bearings.

111

PROJECT 33 ★ *Wheel-Bearing Cleaning and Repacking*

When: Inspect each time you take the boat out, repack when winterizing and at least at the beginning and end of season

Time: 1–2 hours

Tools: Bearing greaser

Supplies: Waterproof wheel-bearing grease

Talent: ★ ★

Tab: $15

Tip: Make sure the bearings are completely free of old grease or dirt before packing

Gain: Extend the life of the bearings, reduce or eliminate need to replace bearings

After all the bearings, cap, hub, and races are clean and the solvent has been removed from them, it's time to pack the bearings with fresh grease.

The grease needs to be packed into the bearing so the grease can get between the rollers and the cage that holds the rollers in place. Forcing grease through the bearing, from the large end to the small end, will make sure it coats the bearings (rollers).

If you have a bearing greaser, place the bearing taper-side down, and tighten the cap of the greaser. Fill the bearing by attaching the grease gun to the grease zerk on the greaser and pumping the bearing full of grease.

If you do not have a greaser, you can pack the bearings the old-fashioned way—by hand. Put a small amount of waterproof wheel-bearing grease in

A new bearing kit will usually come with everything you will need. But often, the bearings you have just need to be cleaned and serviced. Do not clean the new bearings unless you have contaminated them (dropping on the ground, etc.). The new bearings have a light coat of shipping grease that can be left on them. The shipping grease is *not* bearing grease. The bearings will still need to be packed with the appropriate marine grease, even if they are new.

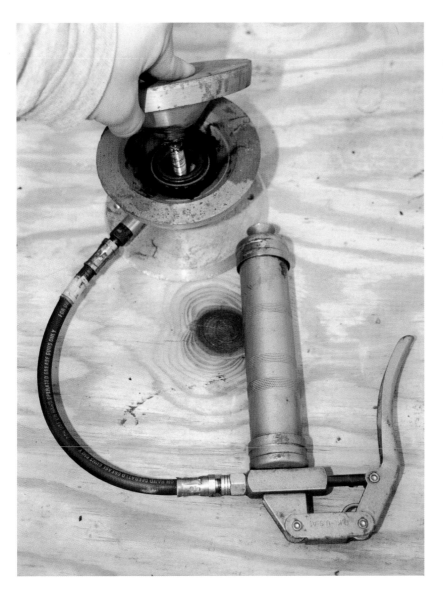

Packing the wheel bearings can be done with a greaser and a grease gun. With this unit, you place the bearing in the device, tighten the lid, and force the grease through the bearing rollers and cage with the pressure from a grease gun.

the palm of one hand. With the other hand, hold the bearing with the large-diameter edge down, and force the large side of the bearing into the grease against the palm of your hand. Keep pressing the large (outside) edge of the bearing into the grease until you have completely filled the internal spaces of the bearing with grease. This will force the grease between the rollers, the inner "race," and the cage. Continue this process, working the grease between the rollers all the way around the bearing. Make sure you complete this process a couple of times. You need to make sure the grease has penetrated and coated the components of the bearing. Clean any excess grease with your finger and install.

It is really pretty easy to get the bearings filled with grease. I like using LubriMatic's white lithium

waterproof grease. There are many opinions about what type of grease to use. One thing is for sure: You need waterproof grease and you need quality grease.

The advantage to the white lithium is the ability to see the grease as you are packing the bearings. If you look at the photo of the hand greasing, you can see the grease being pushed through the bearing rollers and cage assembly. It's easily visible so you can see how much is in the bearing. Its visible color just makes the repacking job a little easier.

Another advantage is that LubriMatic's white lithium grease is very compatible with other grease. If you didn't get the hub and bearings cleaned out exceptionally well, you do not have to worry about the old grease and the new LubriMatic grease separating. It also still offers a very good water washout.

113

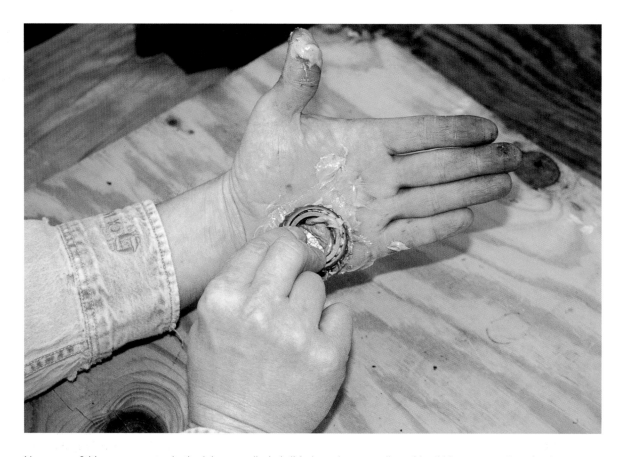

No greaser? It's very easy to do the job manually. LubriMatic makes a quality, white lithium grease for wheel bearings. Put a small amount in the palm of one hand and start forcing the grease into the bearing rollers and cage. The white lithium is visible as it starts exiting the top edge of the bearing. Notice the small spots of grease poking out from between the rollers. Keep moving the bearing around until grease fills all areas of the bearing. When done, wipe off the excess and use it to put a light coat of grease on the race in the hub.

If the grease is not compatible they can separate, or cause chemical reactions that can adversely affect the hub and bearings. The wrong grease could actually cause the bearings to rust and pit, while the grease may lose its lubricating qualities. Check with your local shop to see what the mechanics recommend. They might have a product in your area that works better.

PROJECT 34 ★ *Bearing and Hub Assembly*

When: Inspect each time you use the boat, repair when winterizing or at least at the beginning and end of season

Time: 1–2 hours

Tools: Small hammer or mallet; large pliers; block of wood at least 4 inches square

Supplies: Waterproof wheel-bearing grease

Talent: ★★

Tab: $15

Tip: A block of wood helps to make sure the seal is installed straight

Gain: Clean axle and hub, repacked bearings, prevented failure on the road

After both bearings are packed with grease, place the hub outside (or lug side) down on a clean bench or cloth. Place a medium amount of grease into the hub, along the walls of the hub, and below the races. The axle will need room so you don't need to fill the hub completely. Coat the inside bearing race, if you haven't already, with a coat of grease and then insert the bearing in place. Make sure it fits completely into the race and turns smoothly.

Next, install the new seals. Put a thin layer of grease around the edge of the seal and on the rubber seal itself. It doesn't hurt to put a small quantity of grease on the inside edge of the seal to keep the moisture out of the area. Place the seal, open-edge down,

After the bearing is full of grease, replace it in the race (seat). If you are replacing the inside bearing, put it in place and install the seal. The seal needs to be coated with a thin layer of grease and tapped into place squarely. Do not force the seal in at an odd angle. The best way is to use a small block of wood to keep the seal level. After installing the inside bearing, place the hub on the axle, install the outside bearing over the axle, and push it into the race. Make sure there is a light coat of grease on the bearing race and the axle.

Install the axle nut on the axle and tighten finger-tight, while turning the hub. You want the bearings to be seated fully in the race. Make sure that you installed the correct thrust washer under the nut. The correct washer will be big enough to cover the bottom of the axle nut, but small enough that it does not contact the outer ring or cage of the bearing. If the washer puts pressure on the outer portion of the bearing, it will bind the bearing, stop the rollers from moving, and destroy the bearings and axles. After the nut is finger-tight, turn the nut about 1/2 to 3/4 of a turn more, remembering to align the hole in the axle with the slot in the nut. Pull on the hub to make sure there is no play or movement. If there is, the nut needs to be tightened more. Remember, the nut needs to hold the hub firmly in place, but without binding the bearings.

and tap it into the hub. Use the mallet or hammer, and tap around the edge of the seal to get it started. After the seal is started, a small block of wood can be placed on the seal. Then use the hammer to tap the seal firmly into place and make sure it's even with the inside edge of the hub. Do not push the seal below the hub's edge.

With a cloth and solvent, clean the axle and make sure there is no damage to the axle or threads. Install the hub onto the axle. Slide the outside bearing on the axle and push it into the hub until it is firmly in the bearing race. Remember the sequence? If you have more than one thrust washer, remember to put the correct one on the axle first. Typically, one washer will only contact the inner sleeve of the bearing. This washer will allow the nut to apply pressure to the

sleeve of the bearing, and hold it firmly in the bearing race, without putting pressure on the rollers and cage of the bearing (which would prevent the bearing from working).

After the washer is in place, install the nut. Turn the nut and spin the hub until the nut is finger-tight. The hub should not move in and out on the axle. If it does, the nut needs to be tightened more. Jiggle and wiggle the hub to make sure the bearings are in the races correctly and the nut is as tight it can go by hand.

At this point, use the pliers or a large wrench to turn the axle nut one more time. This time, tighten the nut one-half to one turn more, watching that you align the slots in the nut with the hole in the axle. Make sure that you continue to spin the hub. If the

Insert the new cotter pin, front to back. Bend the straight ends to keep the pin from slipping out of the axle and the nut. The cotter pin keeps the nut from loosening and tightening during use. It's best to always replace the cotter pin with a new pin each time you pack the bearings or work on the hub. Repeated bending of the cotter pin can create a work-hardened or weakened area, and the pin can break at the bend.

Fill the hubcap about half full with grease and tap it into the hub. After it is started all around the hub, place a block of wood on the cap and tap the cap the rest of the way into the hub. The wood helps to even the pressure and install the cap evenly in the hub.

If you have greaser caps, you may have a rubber cap that covers the grease zerk. Clean the hub and remove the cap so that you can inspect the bearing greaser.

If you have bearing protectors or "greaser caps," you can keep the hub filled with grease without disassembling the bearings. With a grease gun filled with the appropriate waterproof grease, fill the hub with grease. Each greaser cap is a little different. If you have a Bearing Buddy cap, the internal section of the cap should be spring-loaded to keep the grease under pressure. As you pump grease into the zerk, you should see the inner section move outward. Stop adding grease after it moves about ⅛ of an inch. If the inside of the cap is all the way out, it probably has too much grease in the cap already.

nut is too tight and the hub doesn't turn freely, you will need to loosen the nut. The nuts are usually installed with a very low amount of pressure, typically less than 20 pounds of torque. Don't tighten the nut too much!

Insert a new cotter pin through the slots in the nut and the hole in the axle. Bend the straight ends so that the cotter pin cannot slip out of position. There are different opinions as to how to bend the ends. Some mechanics will bend the ends in opposite directions around the nut. Others bend both ends outward over the end of the axle, and some bend one end out over the end of the axle and the other in toward the bearing. Whatever you decide to do, make sure the cotter pin doesn't have the ability to move in such a way that the nut can turn. If the nut starts to move or turn, it can wear the cotter pin to a point where it can fail. If the cotter pin fails, it can't keep the nut tight and the bearings in place, setting up a series of small changes that can result in the loss of the hub from the trailer while it's moving. It doesn't hurt to insert the cotter pin so that the straight ends are toward the back of the trailer and the loop end is toward the front. The theory is, if the ends of the pin break off, the general motion of the trailer traveling forward should keep the pin in place.

Fill the hub's cab with more waterproof grease (not packed full, only about half full), tap it back in place to cover the nut, and you are done. After a couple of times, repacking the wheel bearings will be a snap.

Now replace the wheel and tire, then tighten the lug nuts/bolts as tight as possible while the tire is off the ground. Remove the jack stand, lower the jack, and tighten the lug nuts again. It's best to tighten per the manufacturer's recommended torque. If you don't have the specs, many people tighten them with the lug wrench until they have a firm resistance, and then they turn the nut/bolt an additional half to three-quarters more.

PROJECT 35 ★ *Wiring and Lights*

When: Each time you take the boat out, or at least the beginning and end of season

Time: ½–1 hours

Tools: Screwdriver to remove lens from light; small wire brush to clean contacts; Dremel tool and wire-brush bits

Supplies: Electrical contact spray; silicone sealer; petroleum jelly

Talent: ★★

Tab: $10

Tip: A light coat of petroleum jelly around the gasket can help keep it pliable and functioning

Gain: Safety, longer life of the bulbs, fewer tickets for equipment failure (lights not working)

Inspect the wiring from the front of the trailer to the back. Start with the connecting plug and make sure the pins and sockets are not bent, broken, or corroded. If they are dirty or corroded, clean them with a small wire brush. If they are bent or broken, replace the plug.

While inspecting the wiring, look for worn, pinched, or exposed areas that can break or cause sparks that will short the system. If you have any damaged wires, they need to be replaced or patched. A quick fix could be coating them with liquid electrical tape.

Inspect the exterior of the light housings for cracks or damage. If the light housing is damaged, it may need to be replaced, or it might or need to be sealed with a waterproof silicone sealer. The housings are designed to keep moisture away from the hot bulbs.

With the screwdriver, remove the screws that hold the lens in place. Inspect the lens for chips and cracks, and inspect the gasket under the lens for damage. If the lens or gasket has chips or cracks, they can be sealed with silicone sealer or replaced. It's best to replace the gasket with a new one. If you do use silicone, it could seal the lens, gasket, and housing together. Then you might not be able to get it apart in the future.

Remove the bulb by pushing it in and turning. This will release the bulb so it can be removed and you can inspect the contacts of the socket and the bulb.

Boat trailer lights get a lot of abuse. They get rained on, heated up, cooled down, vibrated, and bounced around at 65 miles per hour. What they don't do is spend that much time under water. Yet, they decide to blow the bulb after one dip in the lake. One way to increase the life of the bulb is to unplug the lights when you are submerging the lights and trailer. If the light housing fills with water because there is a leak or bad gasket and then you put the brakes on (you will), the bulb will light up, heat up, and possibly blow out in the cold water.

You can also extend the life of your lights by cleaning the bulb socket with a wire brush, or my favorite, the cordless Dremel tool with a wire brush bit. It's also good to spray the contacts with an electrical contact cleaner like CRC. Remove any dust, dirt, and crud from the lights' housing. Keep the seals around the lens in good shape. Replace the gasket or at least put a coat of silicone or petroleum jelly around the lens to prevent too much moisture from seeping into the housing. You might not stop all of the water from getting in, but if you can reduce it that will help the life of the bulb.

With a small wire brush, clean the bulb contacts and the inside of the socket. This is a great time to use the cordless Dremel tool with a small wire-brush bit. Carefully brush the inside of the socket with the brush and the contacts of the bulb.

If you have electrical contact spray, coat the inside of the socket to clean it. If you have any electrical contact grease, coat the contacts of the bulb and replace the bulb in the socket. Press in and turn the bulb to lock it in place.

Coat the gasket or the edge of the lens with a silicone sealer; or even better, coat it with petroleum jelly to seal the lens and light.

Replace the lens and the screws that hold it in place. Be careful not to tighten the screws too tight or else they will crack the lens.

Before installing the bulb, apply a small coating of electrical contact grease to both the socket and the bulb. Contact grease will help the bulb maintain contact, a good electrical current flow, and reduce corrosion buildup. Again, don't forget to check the gasket or seal on the lens before it is installed.

PROJECT 36 ★ *Trailer Winterizing*

When: Each time you take the boat out, or at least the beginning and end of season

Time: ½ hours

Tools: Jack; jack stands or blocks

Supplies: None

Talent: ★

Tab: $25, if you buy jack stands

Tip: Make sure the block or jack stands are on solid ground. If not, put a flat board of about 2 square feet on the ground first. If one jack starts to settle or sink into the ground, it could cause the trailer to tilt and damage the boat and/or trailer

Gain: Less damage to the sidewalls of the tires if the trailer is on blocks

Winterizing the trailer includes all of the information we have previously covered: touching up paint, repacking the wheel bearings, inspecting and repairing the lights, and checking over the wiring. Additional service only needs to be done when you park the trailer for storage.

Remove the tongue or fold it out of the way. Replace any pins or connectors so they are not lost over the storage period.

After the trailer is parked in its storage location, jack the trailer so the wheels are off the ground and place jack stands or blocks under the axle or the trailer frame to keep the trailer at this level. Keeping the weight off the tires will reduce deterioration to the sidewalls of the tires.

Do not leave the jack as the only support. Jacks can lose their fluid pressure and the tire could end up

If your trailer has a brake system and you are storing the trailer, it is a good idea to check the brake fluid level in the reservoir and look for water. In this case, the trailer tongue is removable so the boat can be stored in a shorter space. That requires that the brake line actually be disconnected.

With a floor jack or small hydraulic jack, lift the tires off the ground so they can turn freely. This will take the pressure off the tires and reduce the sidewall damage that is caused from sitting in the same place for a prolonged period of time.

Jacks can lose their pressure or fluid over a period of time. It is best to block the axles with concrete blocks, wooden blocks, or safety jack stands. After the blocks are in place, remove the jack and the trailer will be ready for storage.

on the ground. Worse yet, one side could drop and the other doesn't, which would tip the boat and potentially cause damage. The boat could slide to one side of the trailer, and the resulting movement could knock over the other jack, and the whole thing could hit a nearby boat or structure.

Make sure that the blocks are on firm ground. If the storage facility has a dirt floor, you should place the blocks or safety stands on a flat piece of wood. The dirt can thaw, become wet, and the blocks or safety stands could settle unevenly in the ground. Small sections, at least two foot by two foot, of ½-inch or ¾-inch plywood will usually provide the support you need.

123

Tool and Supply Checklist

Gallon bucket
⅜-inch extensions, assorted length
⅜-inch ratchet
⅜-inch universal joint
⅜-inch spark plug socket (usually ⅝ or ¹³⁄₁₆)
Acetone or paint thinner
Adjustable wrench
Aerosol cooking oil
Aluminum file
Aluminum polish
Antifreeze (ethylene glycol for the closed system)
Antifreeze, nontoxic RV
Antifreeze, propylene glycol
Applicator pad, polish
Applicator pad, wax
Baking soda
Battery charger
Battery-operated flashlights
Battery-post cleaning brush
Bearing greaser
Brush, carpet scrub
Brush, disposable stiff-bristle paint
Brush, fabric scrub
Brush, stiff-bristle, long-handle parts cleaning
Brush, wire for drill
Brush, wire to clean contacts
Buffing compound
Can opener, for filter
Carbonated cola (pop)
Carpet cleaner
Chamois to remove water
Clean drain pan
Clean soft cloth
Combination wrench, assorted sizes
Cordless drill
Cotton swabs
CRC electrical contact spray
Crest Original toothpaste (non-gel)
Degreaser, spray
Dishwashing detergent, electric
Dishwashing detergent, grease-fighting
Distilled water
Dremel tool, cordless 8000 Lithium Ion Cordless Dremel
      tool bits (wire brush, grinding disk, sanding drum)
Emery cloth
Fabric cleaner
Fabric or vinyl glue
Fire extinguisher
Flush kit, earmuff-style
Fogging oil, ValvTect Premium
Fuel filter

Fuel-proof drip pan
Fuel separator/filter
Fuel stabilizer, ValvTect
Gear lube in bottle or tubes (or bulk lube unit)
Gel coat, Spectrum color-matched
Grease gun
Grease, marine
Grease, waterproof wheel-bearing
Hammer
Hard-plastic kitchen scrapers
Heat gun
Hose, garden-style
Ignition wire set
Jack
Jack stands or blocks
Lug wrench
Magnet
Masking paper or newspaper
Masking tape
Maxi Repair Pack from West Systems
Mechanics mirror, telescoping 2x3
Metal can for soaking small parts
Moisture absorption packets
Mothballs/crystals
Nonskid deck cleaner, StarBrite
Oil, required amount per manufacturer's service manual
Oil-change kit (pump and container for disposal)
Oil filter
Oil filter wrench
Paddle, spreading plastic filler
Paint, bright-colored (or fingernail polish)
Paintbrush
Paint, color-matched touchup for engine
Paint gun and air compressor
Paint, manufacturer's touchup for boat
Paint, model or fingernail polish
Paint, touchup rustproof
Petroleum jelly
Plastic body filler (Bondo)
Plastic dishes to put baking soda in, small
Pliers
Polish, Meguiers acrylic-glass cleaner
Polish/cleaner, metal
Polyvinyl alcohol
Power buffer and pad (or cordless drill with buffing pad)
Primer, metal rustproof
Primer/sealer, rust
Prop shaft grease (as recommended by the manufacturer)
Protective battery terminal spray
Pry bar
Razor knife

Rubber mallet
Sacrificial anodes (zinc in saltwater, magnesium in fresh-
    water)
Sanding block
Sandpaper (80-, 180-, 320-, 400-, 600-, 800-,1,200-grit)
Scotch guard
Scrap wood 2x4x8 inches (pine or oak, depending on
    bend)
Screwdrivers, assorted Klein tools
Sealer, silicone
Sewing needle, curved upholstery needle
Sewing thread (color-matched to fabric), heavy duty
Sewing thread (color-matched to vinyl), heavy-duty
Shop lights and extension chords
Shrink wrap, Dr. Shrink shrink-wrap kit,
Silicone spray, CRC
Solvent, acrylic friendly (Goo Gone)
Solvent, parts-cleaning (paint thinner will work)
Spark plug cleaner (or small wire-bristle brush)
Spark plug gap tool
Spark plugs, new replacement
Sponge or wash mitt

Spray nozzle for hose
Steel wool, fine
Tarp tie-downs
Thread compound
Toothbrush or small stiff-bristle brush
Towels
Used-oil reclamation container
UV-resistant fabric engine cover
Vinyl cleaner and conditioner
Vinyl repair kit
Wax, Kit paste
Wax paper
WD-40
Wet/dry vacuum Shop Vac 1x1, 1-gallon 1.0 Peak HP
    Wet/Dry Vac
White vinegar, household
Winterization kit
Wood cleaner (specialized, depending on type of wood)
Wood oil or sealer (depending on type of wood)
Wood, block of at least 4 square inches
Wooden dowel, a few inches longer than the depth of
    the hub

Resources

American Suzuki
Marine Customer Service
P.O. Box 1100
Brea, CA 92822
www.suzukimarine.com

Bosch Power Tools
1800 West Central Road
Mount Prospect, IL 60056
www.boschtools.com

Dave's Marine and Sports, Inc.
5950 2nd Avenue
Des Moines, IA 500313

Dremel
Robert Bosch Tool Corp.
1800 West Central Road
Mount Prospect, IL 60056
www.dremel.com

Dr. Shrink (shrink-wrap covering)
1606 State Street
Manistee, MI 49660
www.dr-shrink.com

Honda Marine Group
4900 Marconi Drive
Alpharetta, GA 30005-2519
www.honda-marine.com

Klein Tools, Inc.
P.O. Box 599033
Chicago, IL 60659-9033
www.kleintools.com

Martin Flory Group
Public Relations Firm
P.O. Box 360
Gurnee, IL 60031
www.jmaboatpr.com

Mau Marine, Inc.
4771 NW 2nd Avenue
Des Moines, IA 50313
www.maumarine.com

Mercury Marine
W6250 West Pioneer Road
P.O. Box 1939
Fond du Lac, WI 54936-1939
www.mercurymarine.com

It looks like a lot, but in reality, it's not. Many of the products are multipurpose and can be used for more than your boat. The cost to buy these products will surprise you. It's not that expensive to maintain your boat properly.

National Marine Manufacturers Association
200 East Randolph Drive, Suite 5100
Chicago, IL. 60601
Phone: (312) 946-6200
www.nmma.org

Shop-Vac
2323 Reach Road
Williamsport, PA 17701
www.shopvac.com

Spectrum Color
1410 37th Street Northwest, Suite F
Auburn, WA 98001
www.spectrumcolor.com

StarBrite
4041 SW 47th Avenue
Ft. Lauderdale, FL 33314
www.starbrite.com
Tempo Products Company, Inc.
6200 Cochran Drive
Solon, OH 44139
www.tempoproducts.com

3M Marine Trades
3M Center Building 223-6s-06
St. Paul, MN 55144-1000
www.3m.com

ValvTect Petroleum Products
3400 Dundee Road
Northbrook, IL 60062
www.valvtect.com

Wave Publishing LLC.
Sport Boat Magazine Online
Bill Fedorko, Publisher/Editor
www.sportboatmag.com

West Systems products
Gougeon Brothers, Inc.
100 Patterson Avenue
P.O. Box 908
Bay City, MI 48707-0908

Index

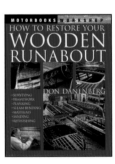
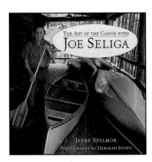
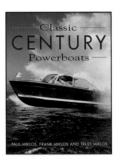

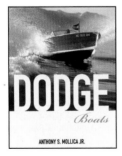
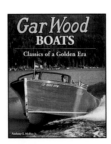
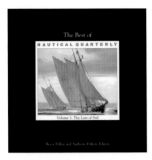